STERLING BIOGRAPHIES

MARIAN ANDERSON

A Voice Uplifted

Victoria Garrett Jones

STERLING

New York / London
www.sterlingpublishing.com/kids

This book is written in loving memory of Chloe Belser, whose own grace and quiet dignity in the face of prejudice served as an inspiration to those who knew her.
I dedicate this book to my children, Katy and Spencer, with the hope that they will always value highly the qualities of courage, faith, and integrity.

STERLING and the distinctive Sterling logo are registered trademarks of Sterling Publishing Co., Inc.

Library of Congress Cataloging-in-Publication Data

Jones, Victoria Garrett.
  Marian Anderson : a voice uplifted / Victoria Garrett Jones.
    p. cm. — (Sterling biographies)
  ISBN-13: 978-1-4027-4239-2
  ISBN-10: 1-4027-4239-8
  1. Anderson, Marian, 1897-1993—Juvenile literature. 2. Contraltos—United States—Biography—Juvenile literature. 3. African American singers—Biography—Juvenile literature. I. Title.

ML3930.A5J66 2007
782.1092—dc22
[B]

2007019268

10 9 8 7 6 5 4 3 2 1

Published by Sterling Publishing Co., Inc.
387 Park Avenue South, New York, NY 10016
© 2008 by Victoria Garrett Jones
Distributed in Canada by Sterling Publishing
c/o Canadian Manda Group, 165 Dufferin Street
Toronto, Ontario, Canada M6K 3H6
Distributed in the United Kingdom by GMC Distribution Services
Castle Place, 166 High Street, Lewes, East Sussex, England BN7 1XU
Distributed in Australia by Capricorn Link (Australia) Pty. Ltd.
P.O. Box 704, Windsor, NSW 2756, Australia

Printed in China
All rights reserved

Sterling ISBN-13: 978-1-4027-4239-2 (paperback)
        ISBN-10: 1-4027-4239-8

Sterling ISBN-13: 978-1-4027-5802-7 (hardcover)
        ISBN-10: 1-4027-5802-2

Designed by Catie Myers-Wood for Simonsays Design!
Image research by B. DeWalt and Susan Schader

For information about custom editions, special sales, premium and corporate purchases, please contact Sterling Special Sales Department at 800-805-5489 or specialsales@sterlingpub.com.

Contents

INTRODUCTION: Song from the Soul 1

CHAPTER 1: Family History 2

CHAPTER 2: Sadness and Joy 13

CHAPTER 3: Dedication to a Dream 25

CHAPTER 4: Disappointment and Triumph 33

CHAPTER 5: Europe Beckons 44

CHAPTER 6: Birth of a Star 56

CHAPTER 7: In Lincoln's Shadow 70

CHAPTER 8: An International Celebrity 83

CHAPTER 9: Applause and Acclaim 99

CHAPTER 10: Farewell 112

GLOSSARY 120

BIBLIOGRAPHY 121

IMAGE CREDITS 122

ABOUT THE AUTHOR 122

INDEX 123

Events in the Life of Marian Anderson

1897

February 27, 1897
Marian Anderson is born in her family's home in Philadelphia, Pennsylvania.

1921
Marian begins to study with noted voice coach Giuseppe Boghetti.

December 10, 1923
Marian becomes the first African American concert singer to record spirituals for a major U.S. recording company.

1924
Marian's debut recital at New York City's Town Hall receives negative reviews.

October 1927
Marian departs on her first trip overseas to study and perform in England.

July 15, 1934
After her Paris debut, Marian hires concert impresario Sol Hurok as her manager.

February 19, 1936
Marian gives her first performance at the White House—for Franklin and Eleanor Roosevelt.

October 1940
Marian begins performing with Franz Rupp as her accompanist; the partnership will last for 25 years.

July 24, 1943
Marian weds Orpheus "King" Fisher, a friend since high school.

1956
My Lord, What a Morning, Marian's autobiography, is published.

August 28, 1963
Performing on the Lincoln Memorial steps once again, Marian sings before an audience of some 200,000 as part of the historic March on Washington for Jobs and Freedom.

October 24, 1964
Marian begins her final concert tour with a sold-out performance at Constitution Hall.

February 27, 1977
Marian is awarded the United Nations Peace Prize at Carnegie Hall.

March 26, 1986
Orpheus "King" Fisher, Marian's husband of more than 40 years, dies at age 85.

January 1910
John Anderson, Marian's father, dies at the age of 34.

June 20, 1921
Marian, age 24, graduates from South Philadelphia High School for Girls.

December 23, 1923
Marian is the first African American vocalist to perform as a soloist at the Philharmonic Society's Academy of Music.

August 26, 1925
After winning the National Music League competition, Marian performs onstage with the New York Philharmonic.

June 12, 1930
On her second trip abroad, Marian meets Finnish pianist Kosti Vehanen, who will be her accompanist for the next decade.

August 1935
At the Salzburg Festival in Austria, Marian meets famed conductor Arturo Toscanini.

April 9, 1939
After being banned from Washington, D.C.'s DAR Constitution Hall, Marian performs for a crowd of 75,000, and millions more via radio, at the Lincoln Memorial on Easter Sunday.

March 17, 1941
Marian receives the Philadelphia Medal; she establishes the Marian Anderson Scholarship Fund for young singers.

January 7, 1955
Marian makes her operatic debut at the New York Metropolitan Opera Company.

July 1958
Marian serves one session as an alternate delegate to the United Nations General Assembly.

December 6, 1963
Lyndon B. Johnson awards Marian with the Presidential Medal of Freedom.

April 18, 1965
Marian concludes her farewell tour at New York City's Carnegie Hall.

July 1984
New York City honors Marian as the first recipient of the Eleanor Roosevelt Human Rights Award.

April 8, 1993
Marian Anderson dies at the Portland, Oregon, home of her nephew, James DePreist.

1993

Song from the Soul

*When I sing, I don't want them to see that my
face is black ... I want them to see my soul.
And that is colorless.*

As the lone figure stepped out in front of the massive
stone columns of the Lincoln Memorial, a great hush
seemed to settle over the multitude of people that
stretched nearly as far as the eye could see. Black and
white, young and old, dignitary and day laborer, with eyes
gazing upward, all looked to the tall and graceful woman
standing before the bank of microphones. With eyes
closed and head held high, Marian Anderson's majestic
voice rose above the crowd as she sang with an intensity
that was spellbinding:

"My country 'tis of thee, Sweet land of liberty . . ."

Marian was praised by presidents and kings for her
exceptional voice, which resonated with a sheer emotional
impact that was unequaled. But for much of her life she was
barred from public establishments because of the color of
her skin. Although uncomfortable with the role of social
activist, Marian Anderson still set an inspirational example
for other African Americans. Grace, dignity, generosity, and
professionalism were her guidelines. A woman of ambition,
she put her career goals first above all else—except
faith and family. Truly an instrument of both song and
inspiration, Marian's was a voice uplifted.

CHAPTER 1

Family History

A singer starts by having his instrument as a gift from God.

The Civil War had ended just thirty years before Marian Anderson's birth, and her paternal grandparents had been among those who joined the swelling tide of black Americans moving northward from the rural South to seek job opportunities in larger cities. Benjamin Anderson came to Philadelphia from Virginia's Tidewater region with his wife and children. They were the first of the family to settle there. Quiet in nature and small in stature, Marian's

Remembered by his daughter Marian for his hearty laugh, strong singing voice, and attractive appearance, John Berkley Anderson posed for this photograph in the 1890s.

grandfather seemed an odd match for his tall and outspoken wife, Mary Holmes Anderson, who was known as Isabella. Striking features and high cheekbones were evidence of her Native American ancestry. Marian's father, John Berkley Anderson, was the oldest of their five children. Tall and good-looking, John had an outgoing and lively personality as well as a fine singing voice.

During the summer of 1895, John, then nineteen, met Anna Delilah Rucker, a twenty-one-year-old school teacher from Lynchburg, Virginia, who was visiting her sister in Philadelphia. Even on tiptoe, the tiny Anna barely

Dressed in ruffled, lacy finery, Marian Anderson was only a year old when this studio portrait was taken in 1898.

reached John's shoulder. The couple fell in love and married later that year. After their marriage, John and Anna moved into a friend's house in South Philadelphia, where they rented a second-floor room. It was here that Marian, the first of their three daughters, was born, on February 27, 1897. (While some documents—such as Marian's passport and driver's license—listed her birth year as 1903, a copy of a birth certificate found among Marian's personal papers after her death shows the correct date.)

This 1897 photograph shows a Philadelphia street bustling with energy and commerce. By this time, Marian's birthplace was ranked as the nation's third largest city, with a population that had already topped the one million mark.

Growing Up in Philadelphia

By the year 1900, Philadelphia claimed the largest African American population of any Northern city, and was also home to many Jewish, Irish, and Italian immigrant families. In her autobiography, *My Lord, What a Morning,* Marian wrote of life in her South Philadelphia neighborhood. "I don't remember being conscious of any difference between me and white children when I was a small child . . . Families mingled on our block and all the children played together." Popular games included jacks, follow-the-leader, and hopscotch. Various Anderson family members—aunts, uncles, cousins, and grandparents—all lived within walking distance of Marian and her parents.

After the arrival of Marian's sisters, Alyse in 1899 and Ethel May in 1902, the Anderson family lived for a time with John's parents. Eventually, they moved into a small rented home of their own. With no indoor plumbing available, Anna Anderson heated water on the stove and bathed the children in a large wooden tub set up in the kitchen. Marian enjoyed sitting in the cozy, warm room, perched close to her mother as Anna cooked and cleaned. Sometimes, as Marian sat at a small bench, she would tap out rhythms with her feet and hands and sing made-up songs. Perhaps this was an indication of great things to come, but Marian later said she was simply enjoying being a child— one who was happy and content.

Anna Anderson (top) poses with her three daughters in this portrait from about 1910. Alyse is at left, Ethel is on the right, and Marian is in the middle.

The Migration North

Following the Civil War, a great migration of African Americans headed northward to cities like New York, Boston, and Philadelphia in search of employment and a better standard of living. Although they were often more highly skilled in fields such as carpentry and blacksmithing than their Northern counterparts, new arrivals usually were not able to find the jobs for which they were trained. In addition, they competed with the North's rapidly growing immigrant population.

In New York City, more than 75 percent of African American men were employed as brick makers, cooks, or domestics (such as butlers). Only a very few held skilled positions such as that of architect or engineer. Women fared somewhat better. Many took in laundry or sewing, which at least allowed them to stay home with their children. Men and women usually worked several different jobs to support their families. Renting rooms to boarders also provided additional income. Some families kept only a single room for themselves.

By the turn of the twentieth century, many Northern cities had large and well-established communities of African Americans that served as support networks for the increasing stream of new arrivals. Between 1916 and 1918 alone, about five hundred African Americans *per day*—a total of some 400,000—joined the **exodus** northward in hopes of a better future.

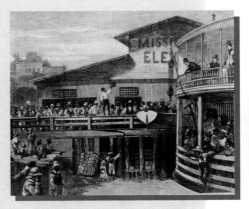

As depicted in this 1879 wood engraving, the docks at Vicksburg, Mississippi, were the first leg of a long journey northward for many African Americans in the years following the Civil War.

During the week, John Anderson worked at the Reading Terminal Market in downtown Philadelphia, selling and delivering ice and coal. Despite the fact that Marian's mother had been a teacher in Lynchburg, she did not have the **credentials** required to teach in Philadelphia schools. Rather than spend the money to further her education, she elected instead to provide care for neighborhood children in her home. Once Marian was born, Anna Anderson devoted herself to caring for her family.

On Sundays, Marian's father served as head usher at Union Baptist Church, one of Philadelphia's oldest and most well-known African American churches. While the girls joined their father, Anna—a devout Methodist—attended another church nearby. It was at Union Baptist that Marian first demonstrated her incredible musical talents and extraordinary abilities as a singer. In South Philadelphia's larger African American churches, such talent was especially encouraged and appreciated, and Union Baptist was no exception.

An Early Love of Music

Alexander Robinson, Union Baptist's junior choir director, is credited as being the first professional musician to appreciate Marian's exceptional talents. In addition to his role at Union Baptist, Robinson was also a director of the Arion Glee Club, one of the most prominent African American choral groups in Philadelphia. When performing with the junior choir, Marian was most comfortable singing as a contralto (the lowest female singing voice), but she was also able to sing parts in soprano, alto, tenor, and even bass—a feat that was highly unusual for someone her age. In addition, her vocal range extended across nearly three octaves (across more than two dozen notes).

Voice Types

Listed in descending order from highest to lowest, the primary voice types are soprano, mezzo-soprano, alto, contralto, tenor, baritone, and bass. However, ranges can vary from one performer to another, and judging a particular voice type can often be very difficult.

The highest female voice is the soprano, which usually extends upward from middle C about two octaves, although sometimes even higher. Next is the mezzo-soprano, slightly lower than the soprano but higher than the alto. The alto extends just a bit above the lowest female voice, the contralto. Contralto voices generally extend upward from the E or F below middle C. Although the terms "alto" and "contralto" are sometimes used interchangeably, true contralto singers—such as Marian Anderson—are quite rare.

For men, the highest primary voice type is that of the tenor, which ranges upward about two octaves from the C below middle C. The baritone falls below the tenor and is the most commonly heard male voice. Below it is the bass, the deepest and lowest type of voice.

Marian *loved* singing for an audience and was very enthusiastic about performing. On more than one occasion, Robinson had to remind Marian not to sing so loudly that she drowned out the other children's voices. Not long after she had joined Union Baptist's junior choir, Marian sang a duet with another little girl in front of the entire church. The hymn was entitled "Dear to the Heart of the Shepherd." Marian sang the alto (lower range) part, while her partner, Viola Johnson, sang the soprano (upper range) part. After the concert, John Anderson told his wife that Viola's voice sounded like "skimmed milk" but that Marian's was like "corned beef and cabbage."

When not performing with the choir, Marian sometimes found it hard to concentrate on her regular schoolwork. While attending Stanton Elementary School near her home, Marian's classroom was next door to the music room. "I was as completely in that other room as one could be while one's body was elsewhere," Marian later recalled.

Since all three of John Anderson's daughters showed an interest in music, he purchased a used piano from one of his brothers. Marian wrote years later, "when it arrived at our house what excitement and joy!" Although money was not available for formal lessons, Marian

. . . Robinson had to remind Marian not to sing so loudly that she drowned out the other children's voices.

and her sisters learned how to play a few simple pieces using a chart propped above the keys. The entire family enjoyed singing hymns, spirituals, and popular songs when they were at home together.

After hearing a performance by a violinist, Marian also became interested in that instrument and vowed to save enough money to purchase one. Scrubbing steps for neighbors, she earned a nickel for each set of three or four steps. She also ran errands and sometimes received a nickel or dime from family visitors. By saving a little bit at a time, Marian amassed the sum of four dollars. (This was a large sum in those days, and is equal to almost $75 by today's standards.)

A neighborhood pawnshop had a violin for sale, but the price was steep: $3.95. Using nearly all of her savings, Marian was able to purchase the precious instrument. Unfortunately, the violin had seen better days, and did not survive more than a few of Marian's unsuccessful attempts to play it. Marian's future as a violinist was over before it began, but her love of music continued to grow.

The Baby Contralto

Marian's aunt, Mary Pritchard, a member of Union Baptist's senior choir, was the first to encourage her niece to sing elsewhere. Aunt Mary would take Marian to other churches and community events, where the young performer would earn a quarter or fifty cents. Flyers, printed with Marian's picture, beckoned "Come Hear the Baby Contralto." More and more people became aware of Marian's musical talent. Although proud of his daughter and her growing popularity, John Anderson

Marian's beloved Aunt Mary (standing) and her strong-willed grandmother, Isabella Anderson, (seated) in this family photo that dates from the late 1800s.

Spirituals

Whether sung alone in a plantation field, at work on a **chain gang**, or during religious services, African American spirituals were created to reflect the joys and struggles of a slave's daily life. The music's rhythm and style suggest its African heritage, and the lyrics convey specific details and messages. Phrases like "the promised land" or "my home" reflected a slave's wish to be free. "Jordan" referred to the northern shore of the Ohio River, where slaves crossed over into freedom. Other spirituals made secret references to the Underground Railroad, a system by which escaped slaves were led to freedom in the North. The lyrics of songs like "Swing Low, Sweet Chariot" and "The Gospel Train" encouraged slaves to "get onboard," "ride the train," or go to a "station."

After slavery was outlawed in 1865, many ex-slaves stopped singing spirituals. They did not want to be reminded of the struggles of their former lives. But by the late nineteenth century, African American spirituals experienced a revival. Beginning in 1871, Fisk University's Jubilee Singers began performing spirituals to raise money for their school. This group is credited with raising spirituals from a simple folk tradition to a classical art form. In the twentieth century, various well-known musical artists, such as Paul Robeson and Marian Anderson, included spirituals in their concert performances, displaying pride in their African American heritage.

Working in the fields or on a chain gang, such as this one pictured from the early 1900s, African Americans used the rhythm and familiarity of spirituals both to unify their efforts and as a source of inspiration.

commented, "I'm not going to have them singing my child to death." There was no need for concern, however, as Marian's commitments were carefully monitored by her mother and other family members. Eventually, Marian was invited to join the prestigious People's Chorus, made up of some one hundred singers from African American choirs all over Philadelphia. One of its youngest members, Marian was so small that the chorus director asked her to stand on a chair for her solos.

. . . Marian was so small that the chorus director asked her to stand on a chair for her solos.

Although the family's income was limited, the Andersons always enjoyed special outings together—such as picnics in Philadelphia's tree-shaded parks. Looking back on her childhood, Marian recalled in her autobiography that a once-a-year trip to the circus was a day-long affair that included a packed lunch and a trolley ride. At Easter, Marian's father would bring home new, gaily decorated bonnets for each of the girls. John Anderson clearly doted on his three daughters. Anna, a former school-teacher, stressed the importance of learning things correctly, telling her daughters, "If it takes you half an hour to do your lessons and it takes someone else fifteen minutes, take the half hour and do them right." When the girls were very young, Anna began to teach her daughters how to sew. It was a skill Marian would use throughout her life.

Unfortunately, the years of contentment and happiness that Marian experienced with her parents and sisters were brief. When Marian was twelve years old, unexpected events brought great sadness into her life.

CHAPTER 2

Sadness and Joy

Mother's influence on us was profound. She did not deliver lectures to us, but she guided us by her example.

Shortly before Christmas in 1909, John Anderson received an accidental blow to his head while he was working at the Reading Terminal Market. He was brought home, but developed a tumor and lived only about a month before dying of heart failure. He was just thirty-four years old. Marian wrote later that she and her sisters "knew that tragedy had moved into our home, and we knew, too, that our lives would change."

John Anderson had been his family's main income earner. With his death, Marian's mother could no longer afford to pay the rent on their small home. At first, she thought the best course would be to take her daughters and move back to Virginia, where members of her family still lived. However, Isabella Anderson, Marian's grandmother, did not want to see her son's family move so far away. She offered Anna and her daughters a place in her home.

Trying to Make Ends Meet

Isabella and Benjamin Anderson's three-story row house was not large. In addition to Anna and her daughters, the structure was also home to several other family members and usually one or two boarders. Despite

This 1909 photo shows women workers at a Tampa, Florida, cigar company. After the death of her husband, Anna Anderson sought similar employment at Newman and Mayer, a Philadelphia tobacco factory.

the reduction in privacy and space, Anna Anderson was grateful to have a home for herself and daughters. In order to contribute to the household income, Anna took in laundry and found a job at a tobacco factory. Later, she worked as a cleaning woman at Wanamaker Department Store in downtown Philadelphia. Anna also cooked meals for the entire family on most of her days off. Marian and her sisters helped, too, delivering bundles of cleaned laundry to their mother's customers.

In the months immediately following her father's death, Marian grew very close to her grandfather. Although usually quiet and unassuming, Benjamin Anderson did not hesitate to stand up to his wife when he disagreed with something she said or did. Marian admired her grandfather for taking a stand for things that were important to him. She would remember his determination throughout her entire life.

Despite living in a predominantly Baptist household, Benjamin Anderson practiced Judaism. "In his religion he observed Saturday as his Sabbath, spent the whole day at the Temple, and referred to himself as a Black Jew," Marian later recalled. "The words **'Passover'** and 'unleavened bread' I heard first from his lips." Sadly, Marian's time with her grandfather was cut short by his death just a year after his

Benjamin Anderson, Marian's grandfather, departed from his family's Baptist traditions and attended Jewish services at a Philadelphia storefront. He observed Passover (Pesach) with similar Jewish symbols as shown here: unleavened bread (matzo) and wine from the Kiddush cup.

Black Jews

William S. Crowdy, a former cook with the Santa Fe Railroad, is credited with forming the first congregation of Black Jews in Philadelphia in 1899. Preaching from a street corner and then later a storefront, the dynamic Crowdy eventually counted some 1,300 members of the Church of God and Saints of Christ.

Despite his congregation's somewhat "Christian-sounding" name, Crowdy was firm in his belief that all Jews were once black and that African Americans were **descendants** of the **"lost tribes" of Israel**. Crowdy's doctrine, which also incorporated a strong emphasis on community and family values, appealed to former slaves and freedmen such as Benjamin Anderson, returning to them a sense of pride and self-confidence that had been lost during years of servitude.

Referring to themselves as Israelites or Hebrews, male worshipers donned the traditional yarmulke (skullcap) during services, while women dressed in long white gowns and head coverings. The Saturday Sabbath was observed, as well as traditional Jewish holidays like Passover.

Although Crowdy died in 1908, the Church of God and Saints of Christ still has numerous followers throughout the United States, Jamaica, and Africa. Today, Crowdy's thirty-six-year-old great-grandson serves as the church's spiritual head.

African American participation in Jewish traditions dates to the early 20th century. Different groups of Black Jews arose out of these traditions. Here, members of New York City's Beth Elohim Congregation read scrolls as part of their study of Judaism.

son's. The Andersons now became a multigenerational family of women with no primary wage earner.

The struggle to keep the family together became harder, but the Anderson women were determined to succeed. In the years that followed, the family moved from one South Philadelphia rental property to another—always trying to find a house small enough to afford but large enough to accommodate boarders, who were important components of the family's overall income.

The Andersons now became a multigenerational family of women with no primary wage earner.

As Marian grew older, relatives encouraged her mother to send her daughter out to find work. But Anna resisted. She thought getting a good education was the most important task for her three daughters. Anna was willing to work several jobs to see that her girls did not have to leave school. Unfortunately, when it came time for Marian to enter high school, Anna made the difficult decision to suspend Marian's education—at least for a time. The money for additional school expenses simply was not there.

At fifteen, Marian left school and began doing domestic work near her home. Marian had never been much of a scholar, so she did not feel especially saddened by her mother's decision.

But Anna was deeply troubled. There was no interruption in Marian's singing, however—especially since she now earned a significant amount for many of her performances. In some cases, she was paid as much as five dollars (which amounts to nearly $100 by today's standards). Even though Marian loved to sing, she also felt a true sense of responsibility to make sure she contributed to her family's income. With each five dollars she earned, Marian only kept one for herself, giving each sister a dollar, and her mother two.

Growing Musically

While still in her teens, Marian was invited to join Union Baptist's senior (adult) choir. Although she still sang with the junior choir on occasion, performing with the older choir gave her the opportunity to sing more advanced and varied music. By now her musical talent was well-known throughout Philadelphia's African American community. While she was performing with the

In this photo taken in her late teens, Marian's serious expression seems to reflect the personal struggles the young singer faced as she juggled challenging academics and a rapidly expanding concert schedule.

choirs at Union Baptist, Marian's talent was noticed by Roland Hayes, an internationally known African American tenor. Hayes and others encouraged Marian to broaden her horizons, and she began to perform in out-of-town concerts. Many of these performances were at churches or small colleges throughout the Northeast.

Aware of the Anderson family's difficult financial situation, the Union Baptist Church congregation took up a collection and raised $17.02 (more than $300 by today's standards) for Anna Anderson to spend on her daughter. Marian, who never missed a Sunday at church, was deeply touched by her fellow church members' generosity. Talking it over, mother and daughter

Roland Hayes (1887–1977)

Born in Georgia to former slaves, Roland Hayes went on to become a highly acclaimed concert performer and the first African American tenor to earn an international reputation. While singing in the church choir, Hayes was introduced to the music of the great Italian tenor Enrico Caruso. "That opened the heavens for me," recalled Hayes. "The beauty of what could be done with the voice just overwhelmed me."

Hayes went on to study music at Fisk University, in Nashville, Tennessee, one of the country's first African American universities. While there, he began to appear with the Fisk Jubilee Singers, a group credited with the transformation of African American spirituals from a folk to a classical art form. Hayes later served as his own promoter and agent in Boston, arranging bookings at churches, colleges, and other concert venues such as Boston's Symphony Hall.

In 1920, Hayes sailed for Europe, where a recital for Britain's royalty led to well-received concerts in various European cities. Over the next several decades, Hayes continued to perform in Europe and the United States. Throughout his long life, he provided encouragement and support to many young African American performers, among them Marian Anderson.

Roland Hayes, in a 1954 portrait, was the first internationally acclaimed African American tenor and an early supporter of Marian Anderson.

decided that what Marian really needed was an evening gown to wear at her performances. After looking at department store dresses and seeing how expensive they were—some as much as fifteen dollars—the pair decided instead to purchase material and make a dress on Anna's sewing machine. The end result cost considerably less than anything they had seen in a store. Marian wore the home-sewn white satin gown for many performances, and both she and her mother were pleased with their thriftiness.

Fearing that Marian's talent and abilities might go to waste without further instruction, the congregation of Union Baptist eagerly took up the cause of finding a way to pay for formal voice lessons for "their Marian." The young singer was very interested in attending a local music school, and church members pledged to finance the tuition. At last, Marian's dream to further her musical education looked as though it would come true.

Facing Prejudice

Filled with eager anticipation, Marian went to the school and stood in line with other applicants waiting to fill out an enrollment form. As the line moved forward and Marian came to the office window where information was being handed out, the young blond woman behind the counter simply looked past Marian to the person in line behind her. Uncertain of what to do, Marian remained standing at the front until the line of new students had disappeared. Only then did the clerk speak to her. In an unkind voice, she asked, "What do *you* want?" Calmly and politely, Marian requested enrollment forms and other course information. "We

. . . the young blond woman behind the counter simply looked past Marian to the person in line behind her.

Marian's experiences with racial discrimination certainly were not unique. In 1948, this Maryland business makes its service policy known—with a sign directing African American customers to the rear entrance.

don't take colored!" was the clerk's cold reply. Marian was dumbstruck. "It was as if a cold, horrifying hand had been laid on me," she recalled years later. "I turned and walked out."

While Marian was not totally unaware of the existence of **prejudice**, this was her first real experience with its blunt reality—and she experienced it in the last place she had expected. Years later, in her autobiography, Marian recalled that, even as a young child, she had some awareness of **racial discrimination**. Sometimes Marian and her mother stood in line longer than other people did before they were waited on in a store. On occasion, the trolley simply passed them by when they stood on a street corner.

There were some sections of Philadelphia to which Marian and her family did not travel, and some social events they did not attend. However, the Andersons, wrote Marian, "were interested in neither the places nor the people who did not want us." But despite her previous experiences with prejudice, Marian nonetheless walked away from her experience at the music school office with a different perspective on what might lie ahead for her as an African American pursuing a career as a professional singer. Fortunately for future generations of music lovers, Marian did not give up. Despite her concerns about what the future might hold in the way of disappointments, Marian Anderson had inherited from her mother—the quiet and small Anna Anderson—a strength of determination and faith.

Musical Studies

Luckily, Marian was able to begin formal music studies elsewhere. A family friend, John Thomas Butler, introduced her to the woman who would become her first voice teacher. Mary Saunders Patterson was a well-known African American soprano. She lived only a few blocks from the Andersons and gave voice lessons to promising young performers. Patterson also welcomed African American artists visiting Philadelphia into her home. Impressed by Marian's obvious talent—and aware of the Andersons' limited finances—Patterson agreed to forgo her dollar-per-lesson fee for Marian.

In addition to learning about vocal technique and how to project and control her voice, Marian studied a range of music beyond the hymns and spirituals of her childhood. Patterson introduced her to new melodies, operatic arias (songs written for

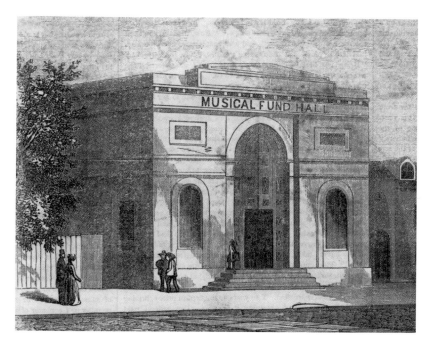

Philadelphia's Musical Fund Hall, shown in this late 19th-century engraving, was the site of Marian's benefit concert in June 1915. The hall was also the location for the country's first Republican Party national convention and host to famous lecturers such as Charles Dickens.

a single voice), and music from Germany, France, and Italy. Many of these songs were performed in their native language. For Marian, it was like a banquet of music.

After several months of study, Patterson felt Marian was ready for more advanced instruction. Once again, her supporters stepped forward to help. A "Popular Benefit Concert to Assist in Musical Education of Miss Marian E. Anderson" took place on June 23, 1915, in Philadelphia's Musical Fund Hall. Both Marian and her Aunt Mary sang in the program, as well as members of the People's Choral Society. The $250 (a sum equivalent to about $4,500 by today's standards) in proceeds from the event went a long way. The money not only funded voice lessons with a new teacher, but enabled Marian to attend high school and resume her formal education.

Although music was the focal point of her life, Marian was very aware of her responsibilities to her family and how she might contribute to the household income once she graduated. Keeping this in mind, she decided to attend William Penn High School, which had a strong secretarial program but few African American students. (A business career was not in Marian's future, however. After spending three years unsuccessfully trying to master typing, bookkeeping, and other such courses, she eventually transferred to a different high school.)

> *Marian was very aware of . . . how she might contribute to the household income once she graduated.*

Outside of school, Marian began to study with her new voice teacher, Agnes Reifsnyder. A contralto and pianist, Reifsnyder taught a weekly class in voice culture. She was also one of only a few white voice teachers in Philadelphia who was willing to teach black students. Under Reifsnyder's instruction, Marian prepared for her first solo performances and regularly began to appear onstage in Philadelphia, as well as in Boston and New York City.

CHAPTER 3

Dedication to a Dream

None of us is responsible for the complexion of his skin.

In 1917, Marian was invited to perform at a gala year-end folk music concert in Savannah. The event was to be held at Georgia State Industrial College, a school for African American students. Since Marian was still in high school, Anna Anderson decided to accompany her daughter on the overnight trip by train. The journey not only marked Marian's first visit to the Deep South, but—unfortunately—also served as her introduction to the humiliating Jim Crow laws that upheld that region's doctrine of racial discrimination and **segregation**.

Segregated drinking fountains symbolize the racial inequalities once dominant in the American South. From pools to pool halls, sports to schools, transportation to telephone booths, lines were literally drawn to separate blacks and whites.

Meeting Jim Crow

After a comfortable ride from Philadelphia, mother and daughter changed trains in Washington, D.C. Once back onboard, the Andersons and their baggage were taken to the first coach. Here, a world of difference awaited them. The car was filthy, with poor lighting and little ventilation. Raising the compartment's dirty windows in the hopes of fresh air brought in smoke and soot from the engine directly ahead. Writing of the journey years later, Marian said, "I had heard about Jim Crow, but meeting it bit deeply into the soul."

Southern hospitality was restored when Marian and Anna arrived in Savannah and were met by the program's hosts. Despite a highly acclaimed performance in front of a racially mixed audience of nearly a thousand, Marian's equally dismal return trip home and the bleak acceptance of fellow passengers riding in the "Jim Crow car" remained more prominently in her memory. Future performances in the South reinforced Marian's intense aversion to segregation and racial discrimination.

Treated as second-class citizens, African Americans were expected to maintain "racially correct behavior," or possibly pay with their lives. It wasn't until 1954 that the Supreme Court ruled in *Brown v. the Board of Education of Topeka* that public school segregation was unconstitutional. This historic decision and its impact on civil rights eventually spelled doom for the Jim Crow laws.

In the fall of 1918, Marian left her unhappy experiences at William Penn High School behind and transferred to South Philadelphia High School for Girls. The school, which had been open only a short time, was founded to support the surrounding neighborhood's population of immigrant and African American families. Its first principal, Dr. Lucy Langdon Wilson, was a

Jim Crow Laws

From the post-Civil War period until well into the 1960s, the term Jim Crow became a **derogatory** symbol for the racial inequality commonly practiced throughout the American South. The term originated from nineteenth-century minstrel shows that featured a singing and dancing slave (portrayed by white actors with their faces painted black) and reinforced the stereotype of African Americans as uneducated and inferior to whites.

Formally clad African American "pallbearers" march in a symbolic 1944 funeral held in protest against racial discrimination and the unfair practices of Jim Crow laws.

Jim Crow laws enforced racial segregation, restricting African Americans trying to maintain self-respect while struggling for basic civil rights. Discriminatory legislation affected schools, sports fields, hotels, theatres, eateries, stores, and more. Some examples from specific Jim Crow laws were:

- No colored barber shall serve as a barber to white women or girls. (Georgia)
- Books shall not be interchangeable between the white and colored schools, but shall continue to be used by the race first using them. (North Carolina)
- Any public hall, theatre, opera house, motion picture show, or place of public entertainment which is attended by both white and colored persons shall separate the white race and the colored race. (Virginia)

Marian (second from the left, in the second-to-last row) poses with her 1921 graduating class from the South Philadelphia High School for Girls.

pioneer in the field of secondary education. Marian, already twenty-one, was several years older than most of her fellow students. To them, she appeared shy and ill at ease. Sensing Marian's lack of confidence in her academic abilities, Lucy Wilson took the young woman under her wing. Although Marian benefited from the principal's guidance and interest, she often had difficulty juggling her academic studies and growing performance schedule—the latter resulting in many missed school days.

Romance

One of Marian's performances while she was still in high school was at a benefit concert in Delaware. After the event, Marian attended a reception where she met Orpheus "King"

Fisher, a young architecture student from a socially prominent Wilmington family. Tall and handsome, King came from a racially mixed Caribbean and European background. (His skin was so light-colored that he was often assumed to be white.)

Although King's older brother Leon had first expressed an interest in dating Marian, it was to King the young singer felt a strong bond of attraction. After dating fairly seriously for a time, King began to drop hints to Marian about marriage, but she had no real interest in anything other than pursuing her musical career.

Although Marian cared deeply for King, her future as a performer was more important. She later recalled, "One gets swept up in a career, and one has time for little else." Although Marian repeatedly turned down King's proposals, he continued to care for her. Despite many future changes, Marian and King would sustain a caring and respectful relationship throughout their lives.

> *"One gets swept up in a career, and one has time for little else."*

Also around this same time period, another man named "King" had also begun to figure prominently in Marian's life. William (known to all as Billy) King was a popular **accompanist** and choir director. Close in age to Marian, Billy King was slight in build with a pleasant and engaging personality. Although not from a musical background, he had begun to study the piano when he was very young. Soon, his obvious talent was noticed by others. By age eighteen, Billy was already a well-known performer and accompanist in the Philadelphia area.

One evening, Marian was scheduled to perform a few songs at the local YWCA, but when she sat down at the piano, a slim young man approached her to ask if he could accompany her. It was Billy King. Marian was deeply flattered by his interest. "I don't know how I got through the next number, I was so excited that Billy King had offered to play for me," Marian later wrote of the evening. "When I got home that night I was still walking on air. I didn't sleep a wink." Soon, Billy began to appear with Marian more and more often at her performances. Eventually, he became her first regular accompanist. While Billy did not share Marian's drive to pursue a musical career above all else, they still worked well together. Their partnership would eventually span thirteen years.

Looking for a New Teacher

While at South Philadelphia High School, Marian continued to struggle somewhat academically. However, she had established a close relationship with Dr. Wilson, the school's principal. Well aware of Marian's musical talent, Wilson encouraged her pupil's choice of a professional singing career. Knowing that Marian's vocal instruction with Agnes Reifsnyder had ended some time earlier, Wilson and other members of the Philadelphia musical community began to arrange **auditions** for Marian in the hopes of finding her another, more advanced, instructor. Once again, the Anderson family's limited finances stood in the way of several options. Despite this situation, Wilson continued to support the search.

Once again, the Anderson family's limited finances stood in the way of several options.

Although a more permanent vocal instruction arrangement was still uncertain, in the summer of 1919 Marian applied for and was granted a scholarship to attend a six-week program of operatic study at the Chicago Conservatory of Music. During her weeks in Chicago, Marian had the opportunity to perform at a

National Association of Negro Musicians

Established to support the careers of black musicians and to promote and encourage the preservation of African American musical traditions, the National Association of Negro Musicians (NANM) was founded in Chicago in 1919. Coordinating a national training program for concert musicians through schools such as Alabama's Tuskegee University and Washington, D.C.'s Dunbar High School, the NANM provided financial assistance and awards to countless numbers of aspiring African American performers. Among them was Marian Anderson, the organization's first scholarship recipient.

Annual conventions are held in different cities each year and feature seminars, lectures, and workshops on everything from arts management to teaching techniques, classical music to folk traditions, and jazz to gospel. Convention performances showcase nationally acclaimed musicians as well as ambitious novices. Nearly ninety years after its founding, the NANM is still going strong, with branches located coast-to-coast throughout the United States.

concert honoring the newly formed National Association of Negro Musicians (NANM). Although Marian felt somewhat intimidated by the obvious talent and experience of the other students attending the operatic study program, her extraordinary gift was obvious to fellow musicians attending the concert.

Throughout the upcoming school year, Lucy Wilson and other supporters continued to arrange auditions for Marian with a variety of voice teachers, always working around her busy performance schedule. Not long before Marian's graduation, the suggestion was made that she audition for the highly respected vocal instructor Giuseppe Boghetti, who had studios in both Philadelphia and New York.

An appointment was made, and Wilson accompanied Marian to her audition. At first, the meeting did not go well. Boghetti immediately made it plain that he was only listening to Marian as a favor, that he was *very* busy, that his time was *very* precious, and that he could only spare a half hour. Wilson bristled at Boghetti's brusque manner, and Marian felt intimidated by Boghetti's bluntness. She was quite nervous as she began her audition. Without looking at Boghetti once, Marian sang the moving African American spiritual "Deep River." Amazed by the young performer's talent, Boghetti reportedly was moved to tears. Finally, he spoke: "I will make room for you right away."

Amazed by the young performer's talent, Boghetti reportedly was moved to tears.

CHAPTER 4

Disappointment and Triumph

The faith and confidence of others in me have been like shining, guiding stars.

The beginning of Marian's course of instruction with Giuseppe Boghetti coincided with her graduation from high school. She was twenty-four years old and anxious to move ahead with her voice lessons and career in music. At their first meeting, Boghetti told the singer, "I will need only two years with you. After that, you will be able to go anywhere and sing for anybody."

Although Boghetti enthusiastically welcomed Marian as a student, finances were again a problem. The people of Union Baptist Church stepped forward once more, this time organizing a benefit concert. Among the performers was Roland Hayes, who had continued his support of Marian's career. A notice about the concert appeared in the *Philadelphia Tribune*: "A committee of public spirited ladies has organized for the purpose of providing a scholarship to enable Miss Marian Anderson to complete her musical education." The event brought in nearly $600—enough for Marian to start her instruction with Boghetti. Although there would be times over the years to come when Marian had no money for lessons, Boghetti never pressed her, waiting instead for her to pay him when she could.

Giuseppe Boghetti (1896–1941)

Of Russian-Jewish descent, Joe Bogash was born in Philadelphia in 1896. As a young man, he traveled to Europe to study opera at Milan's Royal Conservatory. While overseas, he changed his name to Giuseppe Boghetti. Unfortunately, a hoped-for career as a tenor in Europe never took off, so Boghetti returned to the United States after World War I and began teaching voice at studios in New York and Philadelphia. As a teacher, he could be stern and demanding. Marian's first meeting with him highlighted a disposition that could be prickly at times.

Despite his somewhat gruff demeanor, Boghetti was intensely committed to his pupils. He always had a highly competent accompanist available in his studio during lessons, and students performing music written in another language were instructed by Boghetti himself or by a tutor.

Despite a somewhat uncomfortable start with his star pupil, Boghetti continued as Marian's instructor for a large portion of the singer's career. He would remain her trusted friend and advocate until his death in 1941.

Voice coach Giuseppe Boghetti, shown with his most famous pupil in the 1940s.

This late-19th-century engraving shows the type of accommodations most white travelers enjoyed while traveling by train. African Americans, especially in the South, rarely experienced the same level of comfort.

More Work on the Road

Now that school and the pressure to keep up with her academic studies had ended, Marian was able to schedule more performances and travel more often. With Billy King as her accompanist, she began to venture farther away from Philadelphia. Once again, Jim Crow reared its ugly head on travels throughout the South. At first either Marian or Billy made their travel arrangements. They quickly learned that a lot depended upon which ticket agent was behind the window. Once on the train, they might be denied sleeping berths, despite having reservations. A common trick was to sell African Americans tickets for "Berth 13." No such berth existed. Despite having paid the higher reservation cost, passengers were directed to a dismal drawing room, where they had to sit up all night on uncomfortable seats rather than being allowed to sleep in a berth. Eventually, a fellow Philadelphian and music lover named Mr. Ross offered to make all of the pair's travel arrangements for them. After booking everything for an entire tour, Mr. Ross would then alert Marian and Billy to possible rough travel spots. Since Southern hotels did not accept African American guests, accommodations for the duo ranged from college guesthouses to private homes.

With the money Marian earned from her increasingly busy schedule of performances, she was able to save enough to help her family make a down payment on a small home. Located not far from Marian's grandmother, the house had two bedrooms and two levels. The Andersons purchased furniture and made arrangements to have some refurbishing work done—including installing hardwood floors, enlarging the kitchen, and converting an upstairs bathroom into a small studio for Marian. The family remained there for many years.

Learning Under Boghetti

Throughout this time period, Marian regularly attended lessons with Giuseppe Boghetti. The two years he had initially predicted as her lesson period passed quickly, but Marian continued with her dynamic teacher. The work was not easy as Marian focused intently on exercises to strengthen the tone of her voice and her breathing techniques. At times, Boghetti was unyielding in determining what was best for his gifted pupil and her future, announcing, "I am the teacher and shall make the decisions."

Through her studies with Boghetti, Marian was exposed to a greater variety of music, including the works of Schumann, Rachmaninoff, Brahms, and Schubert, as well as British and American composers. Songs might be sung in English, or French, or Italian. And always there was opera. Boghetti, a tenor, sometimes joined his pupil in singing a particular scene. "I might have had my mind set on trying out something else, but he was the teacher," recalled Marian. "And how could one resist the gleam in his eyes as we played at being operatic figures?"

Marian began to learn more about the depth of professionalism required for an artist appearing in public. "You cannot say, 'Tonight I don't feel good and I won't appear,'" she later wrote. "You have to be prepared to carry on even on nights when you would rather do anything else but perform."

> *"You have to be prepared to carry on even on nights when you would rather do anything else but perform."*

A Recording Contract

As Marian's reputation continued to grow, more and more opportunities arose for her. Not long after beginning her studies with Boghetti, she was approached by Joseph Pasternak. Pasternak was the conductor of Philadelphia's Philharmonic Society, a group of highly talented amateur and professional musicians, many of whom also appeared with the illustrious Philadelphia Orchestra.

He spoke to Marian about preserving her moving renditions of well-known African American spirituals for a larger audience. Pasternak was curious whether or not Marian was capable of

This advertising card from the early 1900s depicts "Nipper" the dog, the well-known trademark of the Victor Talking Machine Company (later to be known as RCA Victor), where Marian Anderson made her first recording.

producing the same depth of feeling throughout the repeated "takes" necessary for a **phonographic recording**. After hearing her perform on several occasions, Pasternak was convinced Marian could do it, and put her in contact with representatives from the Victor Talking Machine Company, a recording company that produced records. Marian signed a contract and, beginning in 1923, became the first African American concert performer to record spirituals for a major U.S. recording company. Her first recordings were "Deep River" and "I Am So Glad."

Later that year, Pasternak asked Marian to appear as a soloist at the Philharmonic Society's Academy of Music. Although many well-known performers had appeared there, the Philharmonic Society also promoted the musical careers of upcoming young Philadelphians. Marian was the first African American soloist ever invited, and on December 23 she performed in front of an audience of three thousand guests.

The reviews were outstanding, and both Marian and Joseph Pasternak hoped that her Academy of Music performance might lead to more opportunities with other symphony orchestras. But without some sort of management support for her career, it was nearly impossible for Marian to make the kind of serious contacts she needed in the musical communities beyond Philadelphia.

Disappointment in New York

Around this time, a Harlem concert promoter approached Marian about giving a recital at New York City's Town Hall, to be held on April 10, 1924. While it was an ambitious undertaking, both Marian and Boghetti felt she was ready. They arranged a challenging program of songs—several of which Marian would sing in their native language.

Even though Marian focused intently on practice and study, the months leading up to the Town Hall concert brought a number of unexpected and emotionally charged events. Marian's beloved aunt Mary, who had always encouraged and supported her niece, died suddenly of a cerebral hemorrhage. And Orpheus "King" Fisher, so long a fixture in Marian's life and her only true romance, had tired of waiting for Marian to change her mind about marriage. He announced his plans to wed a young medical student. Despite the turmoil in her personal life, Marian continued to rehearse and prepare.

Despite the turmoil in her personal life, Marian continued to rehearse and prepare.

When the time came for the Town Hall performance, Marian was told that many tickets had been sold and the event would be well attended. Arriving at the auditorium, she felt upbeat and confident. But once onstage, her hopes were dashed. The hall

Town Hall

Originally designed by the noted architectural firm of McKim, Mead & White as a meeting space to educate the public on the issues of the day, New York's Town Hall opened to the public on January 12, 1921, and soon became well known to concertgoers for the excellence of its acoustics and unobstructed seating. With no box seats to block any patron's view, the catch phrase "not a bad seat in the house" originated here.

Long known as *the* place for a musical performer such as Marian Anderson to make his or her **debut**, other famous names that have graced the Town Hall stage include reformer Margaret Sanger (who was arrested onstage while speaking about birth control), poet Edna St. Vincent Millay, undersea explorer Jacques-Yves Cousteau, first lady Eleanor Roosevelt, actress Jane Fonda, and musicians Bob Dylan and Billy Joel, to name just a few.

was less than a third full. In addition, Billy King, her accompanist for the performance, was seated quite a distance away. His physical presence was not there to give Marian the psychological boost she needed in light of the poor turnout. Her courage ebbed, and the performance was disappointing.

To make matters worse, Marian had learned the foreign language songs **phonetically**, without having a true sense of each word's meaning. This gave her performance a wooden quality that lacked the depth of feeling for which she was known. The critics were not kind, and Marian returned to Philadelphia with a heavy heart. She sincerely questioned whether or not she had the ability to pursue a career as a professional singer.

Marian stopped her lessons with Boghetti. "I did not want to see any music; I did not want to hear any; I did not want to make a career of it," Marian later wrote in her autobiography. "The dream was over." Defeated, Marian turned to the individual who continued to be the most important person in her life: her mother. As always, Anna Anderson treated her troubled daughter with understanding and patience, knowing that the young woman needed to take time to think about her future.

Marian stopped her lessons with Boghetti.

Marian slowly began to heal. Knowing how much the income from her performances meant to her family, Marian realized that she needed to make a decision. Anna Anderson encouraged Marian to think of other career paths that she might pursue. But Marian could think of none. She returned to Giuseppe Boghetti's studio, ready to resume her studies. "Then came a time when I couldn't stand it any longer," she recalled. "I just absolutely had to go back to singing."

Triumph on the New York Stage

After some time had passed, Boghetti felt that his pupil was ready to return to New York. It was something she *had* to do, he believed, so that she would truly put the disappointing Town Hall performance behind her once and for all.

Unbeknownst to Marian, Boghetti had entered her name in a contest sponsored in part by the National Music League. The contest's finalists—both vocal and instrumental—would perform with the New York Philharmonic Orchestra during its upcoming summer concert season. More than three hundred vocal contestants converged on New York's Aeolian Hall to audition before a panel of judges. Marian was terrified.

Scheduled to listen to the performances of so many contestants over a short span of time, the judges simply sounded a noisy clicker when they had heard enough. Each singer was given a number—Marian's was 44A. Waiting for the seemingly endless roster of performers appearing before her to finish, she was always aware of the loud clicker that signaled the end of an audition. Sometimes it even sounded mid-melody.

At last, Marian was called onto the stage. Several other contestants had already sung her chosen selection, "O mio Fernando" (from the opera *La Favorita*), so Marian expected the clicker to sound any minute. More and more time passed, and Marian continued singing, her incredible voice resounding throughout the auditorium. Amazed that she had been allowed

As Marian's concert schedule grew, so did her wardrobe. Referring to an evening gown as "my working uniform," Marian felt it was important for her to always look her best when performing.

to continue uninterrupted to the end, Marian heard a voice call from the judges' balcony, "Does 44A have another song?" She certainly did.

Chosen as one of sixteen semifinalists, Marian eventually won the competition and performed with the New York Philharmonic Orchestra on August 26, 1925. Her mother, sisters, other family members, and friends and supporters all made the trip from Philadelphia to hear Marian sing.

. . . Marian eventually won the competition and performed with the New York Philharmonic Orchestra . . .

Wearing a powder-blue gown purchased for the occasion, Marian performed several selections—including three African American spirituals. After Marian's return to Philadelphia, a reception for a thousand guests was held to celebrate her triumph. The "Baby Contralto" had grown into a powerful voice of achievement.

CHAPTER 5

Europe Beckons

If these people believed in me as an artist, then I could venture to be a better one. I could face the challenge of bigger things.

Marian's triumph in New York City resulted in an increased number of concert dates. During the next two years, she continued to perform throughout the United States with Billy King as her accompanist. They had regular tour circuits, traveling to the South, then the Midwest, and then to the West Coast, at different times of the year. Marian's popularity was growing rapidly—especially in the South, where her concerts drew white as well as black audiences. By now, she was earning as much as $300 for a performance.

One of Marian's greatest satisfactions during this time period was her increased ability to contribute more to her family's income. By this time, both of her sisters were working as well: Alyse at a department store and Ethel at a printing company. Anna Anderson was still a custodian at Wanamaker's, but the physical labor was taking its toll.

Uncomplaining even when extra tasks were assigned to her, Anna toiled daily at her job—cleaning, scrubbing, dusting, and polishing. Years later, Marian recalled that

> *Marian's popularity was growing rapidly—especially in the South, where her concerts drew white as well as black audiences.*

her mother's supervisor "was a big person on her job, and maybe she had a heart, but it remained at home when she went to work." One day, Anna Anderson became very ill. That was the last straw for Marian. After speaking to her mother's doctor, Marian called Wanamaker's. With great satisfaction, Marian told her mother's supervisor that Anna Anderson would not be returning to work . . . *ever.*

First Studies in Europe

Despite her many concerts throughout the United States, Marian felt she had reached a crossroads. Her lack of foreign-language study and the ability to truly appreciate and understand the meaning of the words she was singing, particularly those of German lieder—or soulful songs—were stumbling blocks to her career. More than one reviewer, while praising the strength and beauty of Marian's voice, had commented on her lack of depth when singing in another language. Marian began to think seriously about traveling to Europe to study.

Marian now had enough money in savings to support herself for a few months without performing. She made the decision to travel to Europe to study. "I was going stale," she later wrote in her autobiography. "Progress was at a standstill."

In October of 1927, Marian sailed for England on the SS *Ile de France*. Arrangements were made for her to study with Raimund von Zur Mühlen, a prominent instructor in German lieder. During much of her time in Europe, Marian lived at the home of John Payne, a well-known African American singer and actor who had settled in England. Payne, an Anderson family acquaintance, had opened his home to many of the African American performers who had come to England after World War I in hopes of working in a climate free of prejudice.

Unfortunately, shortly after Marian began her instruction the aged Mühlen became seriously ill and could no longer teach. Hoping to find another way to continue her studies, Marian sought out the composer Roger Quilter. Quilter directed Marian to several other teachers, including the well-known baritone Mark Raphael. All offered their various talents to the gifted young singer. Soon she was able to study music in both French and German.

Homesick at times, Marian appreciated the steady stream of letters that arrived from friends and family. A frequent correspondent was Orpheus Fisher, who had reappeared in Marian's life after the failure of his brief marriage. "I am only happy when I think of you," he wrote. "I only get a thrill from my Marian."

During her time in Europe, Marian met many new and interesting people and made friends among her fellow musicians and singers. She was invited to perform in private homes and at

In 1928, during her first trip to Europe, Marian (center) stayed at the home of the well-known African American actor and singer John Payne (second from right).

German Lieder

Emotionally expressive German art songs written for voice and piano, called lieder, address themes such as religion, nature, love, and grief. Although some date from the twelfth century, lieder experienced a strong surge of popularity during the nineteenth century, when composers such as Franz Schubert (1797–1828), Johannes Brahms (1833–1897), and Hugo Wolf (1860–1903) set the poetic works of well-known authors like Shakespeare and Goethe to music.

Schubert's *Die Forelle* (The Trout), for example, tells the story of a fisherman standing on the shore of a sparkling brook hoping to catch a trout. The piano plays a repeating melody that sounds like a fish darting through water, while the singer tells of the fisherman's efforts. Both music and voice set the scene of the story and relay its outcome.

Written primarily to be performed in front of a small audience at a recital or in a salon, lieder require great skill on the part of both the pianist and the singer. They are considered by many to be among the most advanced forms of musical composition.

Sheet music for Franz Schubert's *Die Forelle*, a German lieder that combines voice with music in the piece.

small recitals and, as much as her limited budget would allow, she tried to attend other artists' concerts and performances.

Marian's European Debut

In the spring of 1928, Roger Quilter, Mark Raphael, and others felt Marian was definitely ready for bigger things, so arrangements were made to book London's Wigmore Hall. Although its capacity was not overly large, the site was popular for instrumental as well as vocal performances. Previous artists had included those well known throughout Europe and the United States, as well as young performers just beginning their careers.

Marian joined their ranks in June, when she made her European debut there. This concert led to several other bookings, among them Marian's first appearance at London's world famous "Proms" (the Promenade concert series). Critics, one biographer noted, praised her performance "without reservation." Offers came in from several British recording companies, and Marian was approached about giving a recital to be broadcast on the BBC (British Broadcasting Corporation). A photo of Marian following her Royal Albert Hall appearance was published in London's *Daily Mail*.

At nearly six feet in height, Marian was tall, slim, and quite beautiful. It was not uncommon for Europeans to stare at her as she walked down the street.

Marian's youth and beauty shine through in this image from her first visit to Europe. Far from the prejudices and insults of Jim Crow, the talented singer blossomed.

At first, Marian wondered what was wrong. But eventually she began to develop a greater sense of self-confidence and self-esteem. As an African American traveling in Europe, Marian realized she had more personal freedom than when she was traveling in the United States—particularly in its Deep South. Jim Crow did not haunt her in Europe.

Previously scheduled concert bookings and dwindling finances demanded that Marian return home in late September of 1928, but she hoped to return to Europe again soon.

Economic Hardships

Upon her return to the U.S., Marian resumed her studies with Giuseppe Boghetti. In 1929, she signed a contract with Arthur Judson, a powerful and highly successful concert manager. Marian hoped that by joining the well-known Judson firm she would not only increase the number of her concert performances, but her income as well.

Unfortunately, the experience was for the most part a disappointment. In fairness, the fault was not entirely Judson's. America was struggling with the economic hardships of the **Great Depression**.

A breadline stretches out of sight at Brooklyn's McCauley Water Street Mission as unemployed workers wait their turn for food. A similar scene was repeated in many cities as Americans battled the Great Depression.

Although the amount Marian was paid for her performances did increase somewhat, the number of local managers able to book concerts at her new, higher fee dwindled. In addition, Judson and his associates had no previous experience booking an African American performer, and did not have the existing connections with the small colleges, universities, and churches that had been the main support of Marian's previous bookings. Billy King and Marian had more luck scheduling performances on their own. In the end, they seemed no better off with—or without—Judson's management.

Marian still worried about her lack of experience with German lieder, and vowed she would return to Europe to study the German language as soon as time—and her finances—would permit. The opportunity arose in 1930, when Marian received an award from the prestigious Julius Rosenwald Fund to study abroad. Established by the wealthy Sears Roebuck executive in 1917, the fund had been set up to advance the education of African Americans, especially those who demonstrated talent or leadership in the arts.

> *Billy King and Marian had more luck scheduling performances on their own.*

Marian sailed for Europe in June and traveled directly to Berlin, where she rented rooms from Matthias and Gertrud von Erdberg, an older couple who spoke little English. Immersing herself in the language and the city, Marian also began working with Kurt Johnen, a highly regarded voice teacher. At last she could start her formal study of German lieder.

Marian made her Berlin debut that October. A relative unknown, she was forced to put up the advance cost for the booking from her scholarship money. At the time, it was certainly

While in Berlin, Marian stayed at the home of Matthias and Gertrud von Erdberg, a middle-aged couple who helped the young singer with her study of German.

not an unknown practice for some performers, especially those new to the stage, largely unknown to audiences, or not represented by a professional manager, to have to pay booking and other fees in advance.

"I handed five hundred dollars' worth of American Express checks to the manager," Marian later recalled, "parting with them with the greatest reluctance." The concert was a great success, and she easily recouped her investment. It would be the first—and only—time that the singer would have to finance a concert booking out of her own pocket. For the rest of her performing career, Marian's reputation as a highly talented artist preceded her, ensuring the success of her bookings in advance.

Marian Fever

Shortly afterward, Marian was invited to perform in Norway, Sweden, and Finland. The Scandinavian people, in particular, were fascinated by Marian—an African American with a *Swedish* name. Audiences were smitten. "There was an eager warmth in these people that I shall never forget," wrote Marian.

While on the three-week tour, she was accompanied by the Finnish pianist Kosti Vehanen. They worked well together, and Marian was impressed by his talent and knowledge. "It is not too much to say," she wrote in her autobiography, "that he helped me a great deal in guiding me onto the path that led to my becoming an accepted international singer." Vehanen would eventually become her regular accompanist for all her European performances.

Over the next several years, Marian traveled back and forth between American and European shores. Although she periodically returned to the United States for performances arranged by the Judson agency or Billy King, the economic toll of the Great Depression meant fewer tours, more months of inactivity, and less income.

. . . the economic toll of the Great Depression meant fewer tours, more months of inactivity, and less income.

It was a very discouraging time in Marian's career, particularly in light of her European successes. While in the United States, she continued to see Orpheus Fisher, but would not make a commitment to him—especially with her career virtually at a standstill and the future uncertain. Although marriage and family were not in Marian's immediate plans, her sister Ethel felt just the opposite and married James DePreist, a fellow church member, in the summer of 1932.

Marian's mother, Anna (left), poses with Marian's sister Ethel (right), and Ethel's husband, James DePreist (center), not long after the young couple's 1932 wedding.

Musicians During the Great Depression

The Great Depression hit the United States hard. During the worst years, an estimated 16 million Americans were out of work—about one-third of the country's entire labor force. Musicians and the recording industry were among those most affected. Since money was scarce, few people spent it on luxuries such as concerts or recitals. Although recordings of blues, jazz, and gospel music had increased steadily during the 1920s, record sales plummeted during the Depression years. News reports from Chicago told of unemployed men burning phonograph records simply to keep warm. Although some white musicians still found occasional work on the radio, these doors were closed to African Americans.

Dance bands, however, were somehow able to keep afloat, and many employed black musicians. Eventually, some ambitious African Americans would head their own bands and orchestras—individuals like Cab Calloway, Lionel Hampton, and Louis Armstrong were some of the most famous entertainers to emerge from this period.

This is a 1953 photo of jazz great Louis Armstrong, playing his trumpet.

The following year, Marian returned to Europe once again, this time remaining for two years. She gave twenty extremely popular performances throughout Scandinavia. Based upon the success of those appearances, Marian's European concert manager was able to book more and more concerts for her.

Marian sang her way across the continent, eventually visiting nearly all the major cities—London, Vienna, Budapest, Prague, Paris, Amsterdam, Brussels, and Geneva. Her popularity soared, and her **repertoire** expanded to include more than two hundred songs in French, German, Spanish, Finnish, Swedish, Portuguese, Italian, and English. Admirers sent flowers, and newspapers published photographs and enthusiastic reviews. One reporter dubbed the new phenomenon "Marian Fever."

Based upon the success of those appearances, Marian's European concert manager was able to book more and more concerts for her.

CHAPTER 6

Birth of a Star

I wanted to come home, and I knew that I had to test myself as a serious artist in my own country.

Marian continued to perform in numerous concerts throughout Scandinavia and the rest of Europe with Kosti Vehanen at her side. Her career had now reached its highest point to date. "I sent money home to my family. I bought new evening dresses and clothes . . . I purchased a great deal of music . . . I bought luggage, and gifts for friends," recalled Marian of this time period.

Those that heard her voice were spellbound. In 1933, while touring in Finland, Marian and her accompanist were invited to have coffee and give a brief performance at the home of the famous Scandinavian composer Jean Sibelius. "Before Kosti had finished the **postlude**, Sibelius, with tears in his eyes, came over and embraced me," Marian recalled. "My roof is too low for you," said Sibelius. He then called for a champagne toast to celebrate Marian's talent. Several years later, Sibelius dedicated his composition entitled "Solitude" to the singer.

Marian now began to make plans to fulfill a special dream: to have her mother come to see her perform in Europe. Letters and telegrams were sent back and forth across the Atlantic, and when Marian made her important Paris debut on May 2, 1934, Anna Anderson was in the audience. Billy King had accompanied her on the voyage to Europe. After a warm reunion and month-long visit

Jean Sibelius (1865–1957)

Considered one of the leading composers of the twentieth century, Jean Sibelius is Scandinavia's most famous composer. Born Johan Julius Christian Sibelius, he began playing the violin in his early teens and studied music at the Helsinki Institute and in Vienna. It was around this time that he began using the name Jean after a decreased relative. While Sibelius composed music for the violin and piano, he is best known for his symphonic works. Many of these were inspired by the beauty and folklore of his native Finland. Although

Finnish composer Jean Sibelius was so impressed with Marian Anderson that he dedicated his composition "Solitude" to her.

Sibelius did make a few trips abroad, he lived nearly all of his life just outside the city of Helsinki and was influenced by the works of both Tchaikovsky and Brahms. Perhaps his most famous composition, the hymn-like "Finlandia," was composed by Sibelius in 1899. Even today, its stirring tones continue as a symbol of Finnish nationalism.

with her daughter, Anna sailed back to the States. But Marian remained behind. She was still uncertain how long she would stay overseas before returning home.

A Manager for Life

It was backstage at another Paris concert held later that summer that Marian was introduced to Sol Hurok, a highly successful concert promoter with an international reputation. Although Marian was still technically under contract with Arthur Judson in the United States, she desperately wanted to be free of that arrangement.

Marian was thrilled when Hurok asked to represent her when she returned home the following year. But signing with Hurok meant that Marian was faced with the difficult decision of ending her partnership with Billy King. It was, after all, Kosti Vehanen and not King who had performed with her throughout her European triumphs, and who had been by her side when Hurok came to hear her sing in Paris. The decision was clear: When Marian crossed the Atlantic and headed back to the States, Kosti Vehanen

Marian valued her decade-long partnership and lengthy friendship with the talented Finnish pianist Kosti Vehanen. Here, they are shown during a London rehearsal in the summer of 1934.

Sol Hurok (1888–1974)

Born Solomon Izraelevitch Gurkov to a family of Russian Jews, Sol Hurok (as he later became known) emigrated to the United States at the age of eighteen. Nearly penniless upon his arrival, he eventually established himself as a promoter and **impresario**. He became a naturalized American citizen in 1914.

Throughout his lengthy career, Hurok represented more than four thousand performers and artistic companies, many of them from his native Russia. His clients included pianist Van Cliburn, dancer Isadora Duncan, violinist Isaac Stern, classical guitarist Andrés Segovia, ballerina Margot Fonteyn, and opera singer Maria Callas, as well as ballet companies like the Bolshoi and the Kirov.

Known for his sense of style and showmanship as well as his generous treatment of those he represented, Hurok calmly steered Marian Anderson and her career through the rough waters of politics, race, and finances. Under his careful guidance, Marian Anderson remained a highly successful performer well into her sixties. Hurok arranged recordings and booked performances around the globe, and served as the famous contralto's manager from 1935 until her retirement three decades later.

Impresario Sol Hurok, Marian's manager for three decades, shares the spotlight with his famous client in this 1946 photograph.

would be traveling with her as her accompanist.

King, miserably disappointed and understandably upset, sent urgent letters to Marian. Performing in Europe was one thing, he wrote, but American audiences would never accept the partnership of a white man and an African American woman. King told her she was about to make the biggest mistake of her career. His words angered Marian and their friendship cooled for a time. Fortunately, King's predictions were groundless, and Marian's decision caused little public comment.

Throughout the rest of 1934, Marian continued touring in Europe. Early in 1935, she and Kosti Vehanen traveled to the Soviet Union for the first of two tours there. Her contract with the Russian government specifically stated that she could not perform any songs with "religious **connotations**."

Smiling playfully, Marian holds a snowball while on tour in the Soviet Union in 1935. In addition to concerts in major cities such as Moscow, she also performed in Ukraine, Azerbaijan, and Georgia.

Rather than alter the program of music Marian had planned to sing, it was decided that the interpreter would simply announce the song titles in a different way—for example, "Ave Maria" was changed to "Aria by Schubert." Since African American spirituals were such important components of her repertoire, Marian elected to sing those "as is" and hope for the best. Fortunately, there were no official complaints after her performances. In fact, the Russian audiences were so overwhelmed by Marian's talent that she often returned to the stage for several **encores**.

By late summer, as Marian traveled eastward through Europe after her final Soviet tour, the slow, evil spread of **Nazism** was apparent. An invitation to appear in Berlin had been abruptly withdrawn when the organizers of the event found out that Marian was not "100 percent **Aryan**." And the welcome that many African American performers had experienced for so long in Europe was now less friendly in certain cities. But Marian continued to perform throughout the fall. She also began to prepare for her return to the United States and her new management under Sol Hurok. However, before ending her time in Europe, Marian experienced one of the high points of her career.

Meeting the Great Toscanini

Appearing at a recital in Salzburg, Austria, during that city's internationally known music festival, Marian was told that the famous conductor Arturo Toscanini was in the audience for her performance. "I was as nervous as a beginner," recalled Marian. The dynamic virtuoso came backstage during the intermission. "The sight of him caused my heart to leap and throb so violently that I did not hear a word he said," Marian later wrote. "All I could do was mumble a thank you, sir, thank you very much, and then he left." It was from others who witnessed the conversation that Marian heard Toscanini's words of praise. "Yours is a voice," said the great conductor, "such as one hears once in a hundred years." What higher compliment could Marian receive as she prepared to end her European journey?

Marian and Kosti Vehanen share the stage at Austria's Salzburg Festival in August 1935. Toscanini's words of praise for the singer's performance here would echo across the Atlantic.

After a concert in the Netherlands on December 14, Marian and Vehanen sailed for the United States. Marian had been away from American shores for more than two years. During that time, she had experienced tremendous personal growth as an individual and as a performing artist. She had greater confidence in her own abilities and in her potential for greater career advancement under Sol Hurok's top-notch management.

News of Marian's many triumphs in Europe and Toscanini's words of praise had crossed the Atlantic, and concertgoers were eager to hear the now-famous contralto sing. In a fitting tribute to Marian's considerable success, Sol Hurok booked her December 30 homecoming performance at New York's Town Hall—where, little more than a decade earlier, her recital had received disappointing reviews.

Returning Home in Triumph

As the SS *Ile de France* sailed closer to American shores, Marian looked forward to returning home. While onboard, she and Vehanen rehearsed for the New York concert, and were given a special room with a piano in which to practice.

One afternoon during rough seas, Marian lost her footing while walking down a stairway to her cabin. Falling down several steps, she landed with a thud—and a broken ankle. Despite the pain and discomfort, and a knee-to-foot plaster cast, Marian would not consider rescheduling her Town Hall recital.

Since singers typically walk on—and off—the stage for a performance, the question arose: What would Marian do? An announcement

Following a hugely successful European tour, Marian and Kosti Vehanen sail back to the United States aboard the SS *Ile de France* in 1935.

Arturo Toscanini (1867–1957)

One of the most celebrated conductors of the twentieth century, Arturo Toscanini was known for his passion and intensity, and for inspiring a fierce devotion among those he led in concert. The oldest child of a middle-class Italian family, Toscanini made his conducting debut while on tour in Brazil as the primary cellist and assistant chorus master of an Italian opera company. At a performance in Rio de Janeiro, he was asked to substitute for the conductor at the last minute. Drawing entirely on his exceptional memory, the young Toscanini led his fellow musicians in a highly acclaimed performance of Verdi's *Aida*.

During his legendary career, which spanned nearly seven decades, Toscanini held leading conducting and musical director positions at Italy's La Scala, as well as at New York's Metropolitan Opera, and with the New York Philharmonic Symphony. After retiring from the latter, he accepted an offer to conduct the NBC Symphony Orchestra for a series of weekly radio broadcasts and recordings.

A photo of famed conductor Arturo Toscanini in action.

Suffering from poor vision all his life, Toscanini relied upon his nearly photographic memory when conducting. His interpretations of works by Verdi, Wagner, and Beethoven are considered by many to be unrivaled in their clarity and attention to detail.

could be made before Marian sang, but she felt this was wrong. "To tell the audience I was singing despite a broken ankle would smack of searching for pity, and I was not there for pity that night," wrote Marian in her autobiography. "I was there to present myself as an artist and to be judged by that standard only."

That evening, the curtains opened with Marian standing onstage, her weight on her uninjured foot and her arm resting on the piano. She waited until the intermission to explain to the audience what had happened. The program had been arranged specifically to highlight Marian's musical talents and included songs by Schubert and Sibelius, Handel arias, operatic selections, and African American spirituals.

"Let it be said at the outset: Marian Anderson has returned to her native land one of the great singers of our time."

The audience was captivated. In a review of the concert published in the *New York Times* the next day, Howard Taubman (the writer who would later help with Marian's autobiography) exclaimed, "Let it be said at the outset: Marian Anderson has returned to her native land one of the great singers of our time." Clearly, "Marian Fever" had reached American shores.

On January 16, Marian gave an emotional homecoming performance at Philadelphia's Academy of Music. Many in the audience had followed the singer's career from her days in the choir at Union Baptist. The *Philadelphia Tribune* noted that "hundreds of newspapermen, photographers, and autograph seekers blocked the passage from the dressing room of the star."

One of the world's premier concert sites, Carnegie Hall is aglow with lights in this recent photo. The historic structure was named after industrialist Andrew Carnegie, who laid the cornerstone in 1890.

Four days later, Marian returned to New York, performing this time in front of a celebrity-filled audience at Carnegie Hall. Among the concertgoers that night was Orpheus Fisher, who had had very little contact with Marian over the past several years. The next day he wrote to her, "Marian . . . you really don't know how thrilled I was last evening. Without a doubt I think your concert last night was . . . the finest you have had and I am wishing for many more." Although they renewed their acquaintance, career and not marriage was still foremost in Marian's mind. But Orpheus was a more patient man now. He would watch and wait.

Fame at Home and Abroad

That career was certainly foremost in the mind of Sol Hurok as well, who arranged a busy schedule of coast-to-coast appearances for Marian. In many instances, she shared the stage with some of the best-known performers of the time—including singers, conductors, and musicians—all of whom showcased Marian's talents.

In 1936, she and Vehanen returned to tour again in Europe. They also enjoyed two highly successful tours of South America in 1937 and 1938. In addition to concerts and recitals, Hurok arranged numerous recording and radio opportunities for his

Her face framed in fur, Marian beams at the camera during a 1936 London tour. As war clouds loomed ever closer, Germany closed its doors to the popular African American performer.

Dressed in his Sunday finery, James DePreist, Jr., strikes a confident pose a few months before his second birthday. Childless herself, Marian adored her nephew "Jimmy."

talented client. By 1938, Marian Anderson was earning about $238,000 per year (more than $3 million by today's standards). Whether live onstage, broadcast over the radio, or heard from a recording, Marian's voice was like no other. One reviewer's words said it all when he wrote of "Miss Anderson's power to move her listeners as can no other singer of her generation."

In addition to her well-booked European tour, 1936 had also brought additional excitement to Marian's life. While in Europe, her sister Ethel gave birth to a son, who was named after his father. Little Jimmy and his aunt Marian would enjoy a special bond in the years to come. Also in 1936, Marian was invited by the first lady, Eleanor Roosevelt, to perform at the White House.

Always eager to promote the talents of African American artists, Eleanor Roosevelt had long been an advocate of civil rights. Her stand against discriminatory practices that existed throughout the American South was not a popular one, but Mrs. Roosevelt was unmoved.

In addition to Marian and her accompanist, the first lady also invited Anna Anderson, and personally introduced her to the president. "I shall never forget seeing these two ladies enter the room," wrote Kosti Vehanen some years later. "In all of Mrs. Anderson's being, there was evident the feeling that this was one of the greatest moments in her life." Marian and Vehanen were invited to the White House again in June of 1939. This time the occasion was much more formal—a special recital for England's king and queen.

Marian and Vehanen were invited to the White House again in June of 1939.

But two months before the second White House performance, an event occurred that marked a turning point in history—a point from which there was no going back. Like a large stone dropped into a calm pool, the waves caused by this single incident rippled throughout the remainder of Marian's life and career, impacting the lives and careers of other African Americans as well.

CHAPTER 7

In Lincoln's Shadow

I forgave the DAR many years ago. You lose a lot of time hating people.

It all began innocently enough. In the summer of 1938, representatives from Howard University contacted Sol Hurok about sponsoring one of Marian Anderson's concerts. Located in the nation's capital, Howard was a historically African American institution that had been founded shortly after the Civil War. The request was a

Awarded an honorary doctorate of music by Howard University in June of 1938, Marian dons academic dress for the ceremony. It was the first of some 50 honorary degrees she received during her lifetime.

relatively routine one, especially since Marian had given recitals as part of Howard University's yearly concert series since the early 1930s. It was agreed that Marian would perform during the next concert season, on Easter Sunday—April 9, 1939. The location of the performance was yet to be determined.

In January of 1939, Howard University officials, aware of Marian's soaring popularity, agreed that there was no building large enough on campus to hold the number of people expected to attend the April concert. They began to look for sites elsewhere in Washington.

Constitution Hall, with its nearly four-thousand-seat capacity, certainly fit the bill. The auditorium was owned by the Daughters of the American Revolution (DAR), a patriotic society chartered by Congress in 1896. Home to the Washington Opera Company and the National Symphony Orchestra, Constitution Hall was the largest and grandest of the city's facilities, and appeared to be the ideal location for Marian's performance.

The DAR Says "No"

Sol Hurok contacted the hall's management and requested the April 9 date. He was told that it was already booked. He named several other dates in April and was told, once again, that these dates were not available either. After checking with others in the entertainment field, Hurok found out that the dates in question *were* indeed available—but only to white performers.

Although prominent artists such as Roland Hayes had performed at Constitution Hall in the past, since 1932 the DAR had effectively banned all African American performers from the site. Despite the fact that Marian Anderson had performed for European royalty and the U.S. president, the DAR would make no exception. Even though Washington, D.C., had a large African

American population and was not located in the Deep South, segregation was not uncommon. In 1939, Jim Crow laws were alive and well in the nation's capital.

Hurok—and the officials at Howard University—were furious. As a Russian-Jew who had immigrated to the United States, Hurok had seen his own share of prejudice and discrimination. To treat Marian Anderson, an internationally acclaimed singer, in this way was completely unacceptable. Word soon reached the White House, and Eleanor Roosevelt went into action. She was joined by Harold Ickes, the Secretary of the Interior and a fellow civil rights supporter. After some discussion as to the best course of action, Mrs. Roosevelt made her feelings known.

Noted civil rights attorney Charles H. Houston speaks out in March of 1939 against the Washington, D.C., school board's decision to mirror the DAR and bar Marian from performing at its Central High School Auditorium.

Daughters of the American Revolution

Chartered by Congress in 1896, the National Society of the Daughters of the American Revolution, or DAR, as it is commonly known, is a patriotic association of women who can trace their direct descent from an ancestor who actively participated in the American Revolution. Today, nearly 200,000 women in some 3,000 chapters around the world belong to the DAR. The organization's extensive library is one of the largest genealogical centers in the country. Its museum houses over 30,000 items of historical importance pertaining to eighteenth- and nineteenth-century American fine and decorative arts. Both are located at the Society's three-building headquarters in the nation's capital. Built in 1929, DAR Constitution Hall still remains the largest concert hall in Washington, D.C.

This elaborate ceremony marks an early 1900s DAR convention.

Mrs. Roosevelt Takes Action

As a direct descendant of a Revolutionary War veteran, Mrs. Roosevelt was a member of the DAR. Because of that organization's treatment of Marian Anderson and their refusal to allow African American artists to perform at Constitution Hall, Eleanor Roosevelt resigned her membership. "I am in complete disagreement with the attitude taken in refusing Constitution Hall to a great artist," she said on February 26 in her letter to the DAR president. "You had an opportunity to lead in an enlightened way and it seems to me that your organization has failed. I realize that many people will not agree with me, but feeling as I do this seems to me the only proper procedure to follow."

Eleanor Roosevelt's letter to the DAR announces her resignation from the organization over their decision to bar Marian Anderson from Constitution Hall. The story made front-page headlines in more than 400 newspapers coast to coast.

To further drive home the point, the next day Eleanor Roosevelt announced her decision to resign from the DAR in her nationally syndicated newspaper column, "My Day." The column reached millions of readers across the country. Without specifically naming the DAR or outlining their "whites-only" policy, Mrs. Roosevelt wrote, "I belong to an organization. . . .They have taken an action which has been widely talked of in the press. To remain as a member implies approval of that action, and therefore I am resigning."

Eleanor Roosevelt (1884–1963)

First lady to President Franklin Roosevelt, Eleanor Roosevelt— still considered one of the most admired figures of our time— was an activist, teacher, wife, humanitarian, mother, diplomat, and author. Orphaned at age nine, Eleanor Roosevelt's childhood was a lonely one. With her marriage in 1905 to Franklin Roosevelt, she was thrust into the political spotlight. His subsequent battle with polio brought even more challenges as Eleanor stepped in to keep Franklin's presidential aspirations alive.

Unafraid to speak out in the face of injustice, Eleanor Roosevelt was no stranger to controversy. Although she was born into wealth and privilege, Eleanor dedicated her life to those who were less fortunate. She championed many causes throughout her long and event-filled life. Among these were child welfare, housing reform, unemployment, and world peace, but it was to civil rights that Eleanor turned her strongest focus—taking an often unpopular stand on this very controversial issue.

Eleanor Roosevelt and Marian discuss a magazine article featuring the famous contralto.

The response was astounding. From coast to coast, newspaper headlines appeared, such as: "MRS. ROOSEVELT TAKES STAND: RESIGNS FROM DAR" and "MRS. ROOSEVELT QUITS DAR." A national survey taken in mid-March showed that nearly seventy percent of Americans supported Eleanor Roosevelt's decision. Unsurprisingly, most of those who opposed her actions came from the Deep South.

A Symbol of Her People

And what of Marian herself? Uncomfortable as an activist, Marian's goal remained the same: simply to sing. Many years later, James DePreist wrote of his aunt, "She saw herself neither as a victim nor heroine, simply as an artist who happened to be crossing an intersection of United States history when **racism** collided with conscience." Rather than dwell on feelings of hurt or disappointment in light of the DAR's decision, Marian focused on her music.

She was in California in the midst of a busy concert schedule when the "My Day" column appeared. Although she was constantly bombarded by newspaper reporters asking her for a statement, she said nothing. Marian believed her primary focus should be on her audience. It was up to Sol Hurok to fight the battles concerning where she could—or could not—perform.

Marian believed her primary focus should be on her audience.

And Sol Hurok was ready to fight. Hurok, along with Howard University officials, was *determined* that Marian Anderson would sing in Washington, D.C., even if it meant renting an enormous tent. In fact, the idea of a free outdoor concert began to have more and more appeal, as an outdoor performance would allow a larger number of people to attend.

It was then suggested by Walter White, the executive secretary of the NAACP (National Association for the Advancement of Colored People), that the concert be held on the steps of the Lincoln Memorial. Secretary of the Interior Ickes and President Roosevelt both approved the plan. What better place for an African American singer to perform than at the marble feet of the "Great Emancipator," the president credited with ending slavery.

At first, Marian Anderson was reluctant to perform at the Lincoln Memorial. However, after seeking

Fair hair and blue eyes offered no indication of Walter White's African American heritage. The outspoken NAACP head worked tirelessly for civil rights during the first half of the 20th century.

her mother's opinion and giving it a great deal of thought, Marian agreed. "I studied my conscience," she wrote in her autobiography. "I could see that my significance as an individual was small in this affair. I had become, whether I liked it or not, a symbol, representing my people. I had to appear."

To compound matters further, Kosti Vehanen had become ill and was hospitalized early in 1939. Marian's immediate concern was for the well-being of her friend and accompanist rather than the turmoil that was swirling in Washington. As Marian continued her previously scheduled tour of concerts throughout the United States, Franz Rupp stepped in as Vehanen's temporary replacement. Rupp, a German Jew, had fled the Nazi

takeover of his homeland the previous year. But by Easter
Sunday, Vehanen was well enough to perform again with Marian.

The Day of the Concert

On the morning of April 9, Marian took the train from
Philadelphia to Washington, where the weather was
unseasonably cool and overcast. Her mother and two sisters
accompanied her. The thirty-minute concert was scheduled for
5 p.m., so very early in the afternoon Marian and Vehanen made
a brief visit to the site to check out the half-dozen broadcasting
microphones, public address system, and Steinway piano—the
first to be carried up the memorial's steps. All had been set up on
a platform specially constructed for the event.

Not long after the two departed,
large crowds began to gather on the
grounds of the memorial. By the time of
the performance, a massive audience
extended nearly as far as the eye could
see—an estimated 75,000 people had
turned out to hear Marian Anderson
sing, and millions of people coast-to-
coast listened to the radio broadcast of the concert.

Not long after the two departed, large crowds began to gather on the grounds of the memorial.

Since no Washington, D.C., hotel would allow them to book
a room, Marian and her family spent the hours before the concert
at the home of the former governor of Pennsylvania, Gifford
Pinchot, and his wife. Kosti Vehanen and Sol Hurok joined them
there. The group then traveled to the Lincoln Memorial by
police-escorted limousine.

Upon arrival, officers held back the crowds while Marian and
Vehanen were led through a passageway and into a small waiting
room. Seated on the platform were two hundred dignitaries—

Her back to the camera, Marian sings to a crowd estimated at 75,000—the largest gathering in the nation's capital up to that time.

among them members of Congress, Supreme Court justices, members of Roosevelt's cabinet, and Marian's family.

The singer later likened her feelings at the time to those that she'd had when she spoke to Toscanini several years earlier. "My heart leaped wildly, and I could not talk," she recalled. "I even wondered whether I would be able to sing." But to those who saw her, she radiated a quiet dignity and sincere professionalism. "The arm which I took to steady her," Sol Hurok later commented, "was steadier than my own." As Kosti Vehanen headed out onto the stage ahead of Marian, he remembered that "she stood quiet and held her head high."

A Voice of Change

Not long before, partial cloudiness had given way to brilliant sunshine, with a brisk breeze coming in off the Potomac River. Wearing a long black gown and a mink coat, Marian stepped out in front of the pillars of the vast memorial.

Although her first true glimpse of the multitude arrayed before her nearly took Marian's breath away, she felt that "a great wave of good will poured out from these people." As she stepped up to the bank of microphones, the crowd seemed to hush. Then, in the shadow of Lincoln's great marble image, Marian began with an emotional rendition of "America."

After four more selections—"O mio Fernando," "Ave Maria," "Gospel Train," "Trampin'"—and a brief intermission, she ended the program with the African American spiritual "My Soul Is Anchored in the Lord." As an encore, Marian performed one more spiritual, "Nobody Knows the Trouble I've

As she stepped up to the bank of microphones, the crowd seemed to hush.

Seen." Though she had spoken little beforehand about the controversy that had brought her to the Lincoln Memorial steps on that historic Easter Sunday afternoon, her musical selections said it all as she began with the stirring words of "America" and continued on to songs that spoke of the bonds of slavery and the humiliations of social injustice.

Her performance was broadcast across the country as millions listened on the radio.

The crowd's reaction nearly defied description—cheering, pounding, shouting, stomping. Marian was so amazed that she didn't even remember the brief words she spoke to the audience, but read them in the newspaper the next day: "I am overwhelmed. I just can't talk. I can't tell you what you have done for me today. I thank you from the bottom of my heart again and again."

Standing at Lincoln's marble feet, Marian and her mother gaze up at the "Great Emancipator" on Easter Sunday, April 9, 1939—a date forever etched in the memories of those attending the singer's historic outdoor performance.

Marian Anderson's life would never be the same after her Easter Sunday performance in 1939. Referred to later as "America's first civil rights rally," the concert not only marked a turning point in the lives of countless African Americans but also transformed the attitude of many whites toward racial discrimination.

CHAPTER 8

An International Celebrity

Prejudice is like a hair across your cheek.
You can't see it, you can't find it with your fingers,
but you keep brushing at it because the feel of it
is irritating.

Following the Easter Sunday concert and her White House recital in June of 1939, Marian Anderson and Eleanor Roosevelt crossed paths again in Richmond, Virginia. On July 2, at the annual convention of the NAACP, more than five thousand people watched as Mrs. Roosevelt presented Marian with that organization's highest honor, the Spingarn Medal. The award, given

On July 2, 1939, Marian is presented with the NAACP's prestigious Spingarn Medal by First Lady Eleanor Roosevelt. The two women became lifelong friends, frequently corresponding by letter from around the world.

When illness forced Kosti Vehanen to return to Finland in 1940, Franz Rupp became Marian's permanent accompanist. Seen here rehearsing for a performance, the duo would continue as partners until Marian's 1965 retirement.

annually since 1915, recognizes those African Americans "who perform acts of distinguished merit and achievement." Now in her early forties, Marian was an international celebrity and one of the most popular musical artists in the United States. Her concert schedule included as many as eighty to ninety performances a year.

In 1940, poor health forced Kosti Vehanen to make the difficult decision to return to Finland. He had been at Marian's side through some of the most important events of her musical career, and she would miss him. Fortunately, Franz Rupp was once again available, and he soon became Marian's regular accompanist. Their partnership would last a quarter century.

Kosti Vehanen (1887–1957)

A native of Finland, Kosti Vehanen first met Marian Anderson in 1930 during her second trip to Europe. Vehanen and Rule Rasmussen, a Norwegian concert manager, had been looking for new talent to promote and a mutual friend encouraged them to seek out Marian. Almost immediately, Vehanen was impressed by her amazing talent and ended up accompanying Marian on the piano for an upcoming Scandinavian tour. Neither realized at the time that this tour would mark the beginning of a decade-long partnership and a lasting friendship.

Fluent in Finnish and German, with a strong knowledge of French, Italian, and English, Vehanen was the ideal accompanist for Marian. Together they carefully planned each of Marian's programs. First, Vehanen would write the names of selected songs on individual slips of paper; these slips were then organized into groups and numbered. The end result was the final program Marian would sing.

When illness forced the end of his partnership with Marian in 1940, Vehanen returned to Finland. There he wrote a book entitled *Marian Anderson: A Portrait*, an affectionate look back at his experiences while touring with the famous contralto.

A photo of Kosti Vehanen and Marian on a European tour in the 1930s.

Orpheus "King" Fisher first met Marian while in high school and remained an important figure in the years to come. Despite several proposals of marriage from King, Marian initially opted to remain devoted to her career.

A Life Together

During this same time period, Orpheus "King" Fisher again began to figure more prominently in Marian's life. He was frequently seen escorting the famous singer to various social engagements, and rumors of their impending marriage began to circulate. Marian was thinking seriously about the idea, but hesitated in making a commitment. How would the demands of her busy career mesh with those of marriage? Could she successfully blend the two?

Marian felt that she and King *would* eventually marry, but the question now was *when*. In the meantime, the couple began to talk about buying a home together—one that would provide a much-needed place of retreat for the busy star. Owing to Marian's busy travel schedule, King decided to take on the task of finding the perfect house, but the search was frustrating. He would find what seemed like the perfect spot, only to have the house suddenly taken off the market by sellers not interested in non-white buyers.

Finally, in the summer of 1940, Marian and King settled on a rambling Victorian farmhouse and outbuildings that were located on a hundred acres in Danbury, Connecticut. They named it Marianna Farm, after Marian and her mother.

After several years, King put his skills as an architect to work, designing and building a new home for them on the property. A small studio was also constructed where Marian could practice for upcoming concerts and recitals. Sheep, pigs, cows, horses, and chickens roamed the barn and fields, and a small brook was dammed to make a swimming hole.

Named after the singer and her mother, Marianna Farm and its rolling Connecticut farmland became a place of rest, refuge, and retreat for Marian and King.

Radio commentator Deems Taylor presents Marian with the Philadelphia Medal, also known as the Bok Award, on March 17, 1941. The first African American to be so honored, Marian used the $10,000 prize to establish a scholarship fund for aspiring young singers.

In 1941, Marian was the recipient of the Philadelphia Medal (also known as the Bok Award), presented annually to "a Philadelphian who had done some service that redounds to the credit of the city." With the award came a $10,000 check. Remembering the many people who had come to her aid in her youth, the singer used the money to establish the Marian Anderson Scholarship Fund to assist young vocalists with their continuing studies. Beginning in 1943 and continuing for nearly three decades, annual awards ranging from several hundred to a thousand dollars were given to singers between the ages of sixteen and thirty. Many of the applicants went on to establish highly successful careers as well-known vocalists.

Later that year, when the United States entered World War II, Marian added benefit performances at military bases and veterans hospitals to her already busy concert schedule. Always gracious and dignified, Marian was more than willing to lend her support to the war effort. Her generosity of spirit was reflected on many other occasions as well. Once, after performing at a small college in Nebraska, the famous singer stopped at her hotel's front desk to check for messages. The young student working as the clerk there mentioned how much she had hoped to attend the concert, but that she had not been able to because she had to work. Then and there, in the hotel lobby, without an accompanist, Marian Anderson sang Schubert's "Ave Maria" for the young clerk.

With Franz Rupp accompanying her on the piano, Marian sings to troops stationed at Colorado's Fort Logan Air Force Base in March 1943.

Marian Anderson Scholarship Fund

For nearly thirty years, young aspiring vocalists benefited from the financial assistance of the Marian Anderson Scholarship Fund. Recipients included Mattiwilda Dobbs, among the first African American vocalists to appear at the Metropolitan Opera and the first African American female to be given a title role there. Shirley Verrett, one of the most internationally prominent mezzo-sopranos of the 1970s and 80s, was an award recipient, as was Martha Flowers. Flowers, a well-known opera singer, was also famous for her long-running role as "Bess" in George Gershwin's *Porgy and Bess*. Another winner, Camilla Williams, later became one of the first African American singers to perform with the New York City Opera. Award recipient Judith Raskin, a leading singer first at the New York City Opera and then at the Metropolitan Opera, has been described as "one of the greatest lyric sopranos of the 20th century."

Fewer than thirty applicants entered the competition the first year, but that number rose to more than six hundred in a decade. Competition was fierce. Jessye Norman and Leontyne Price—later considered two of the world's most notable sopranos—were contestants, but did not win. However, even those who did not receive an award came away with advice about future study and encouragement for the future.

Shown here in 1945, Marian especially enjoyed those performances for military personnel "that were less formal and more relaxed than her regular concert hall appearances.

With Dignity and Grace

In addition to her wartime benefit performances, Marian continued her rigorous touring schedule, which generally ran from October into May. Intermingled among these dates were several concerts at New York City's Carnegie Hall, which were usually held in January.

In addition to Franz Rupp, Marian toured with Isaac Jofe, her traveling manager. Hired by Sol Hurok, one of Jofe's primary responsibilities was to handle all scheduling and hotel arrangements in the hopes of sparing Marian some of the humiliations from the racial prejudice that arose on tour. Despite her fame, Marian still suffered insults. It was a credit to her intense professionalism that she was able to overcome them and provide audiences with top-quality performances again and again.

Given the keys to Atlantic City, Marian was refused a room there. In other cities, she might be able to book a room, but had

A smiling Marian poses with her accompanist, Franz Rupp (center), and traveling manager, Isaac Jofe, while on tour in February 1945.

to use the service elevator to get to it. Staying in Los Angeles, Marian was barred from her hotel's formal dining room. In an interview given years later, Franz Rupp told of a restaurant in Birmingham, Alabama, that refused service to Marian but allowed German prisoners of war to eat there.

Upon arrival at one Southern train station, Marian was greeted with flowers, news photographers, and a large welcoming committee. After the ceremonies ended, Marian, Franz Rupp, and Isaac Jofe headed outside to their waiting car, trailed by news reporters and those who had attended the event. Marian was barred at the door by a policeman. She could not exit through the "whites-only" waiting room, but had to walk alone to the "colored" waiting room in order to leave the building. The list of indignities suffered seemed endless.

Some things did change, however. In the fall of 1942, Marian was invited to sing at a benefit concert at Constitution Hall to aid war relief. She agreed, but with the condition that the seating arrangements not be segregated—a first for the DAR. The sold-out concert was held on January 7, 1943. Eleanor Roosevelt, an attendee at the event, noted in her "My Day" column, "It was a significant evening not only from an artistic point of view but from the social point of view."

Although the evening marked Marian's first performance in the nation's capital since 1939, she did not make any public comment that night, preferring again to focus strictly on her singing. "When I finally walked into Constitution Hall and sang from its stage I had no feeling different from what I have in other halls," she later wrote in her autobiography. "There was no sense of triumph. I felt that it was a beautiful concert hall, and I was happy to sing in it." Few might be so gracious under the circumstances, but that was Marian's way.

Returning to Washington for the first time since her historic 1939 Lincoln Memorial concert, Marian finally appears on the Constitution Hall stage.

Marriage and Work

In the summer of 1943, Marian finally agreed to marry Orpheus Fisher. On July 17, the couple exchanged vows at a small, private ceremony at Bethel Methodist Church not far from their Danbury home. Respecting the newlyweds' wish for privacy, no mention was made to the press, and Sol Hurok did not announce the marriage until later that year. Life for the couple continued much as it had, with Marian on the road several months at a time and King tending to various projects at Marianna Farm.

In the years after World War II, Marian began to appear more frequently on the radio and also resumed touring overseas, making her first return visit to Europe in 1949. Prior to that tour, she was treated for a growth that had appeared on her esophagus. Despite the potential risk to her vocal chords, surgery was a must. The delicate procedure was performed and a benign (not dangerous) cyst was removed. After a period of rest, Marian was back to performing with no ill effects. In the 1940s and early 1950s, her concert stops included Tunisia, Morocco, Israel, South America, Jamaica and the West Indies, Scandinavia, and Japan and the Far East.

Marian Anderson and Orpheus Fisher pose at Marianna Farm on their wedding day—July 17, 1943. The marriage, the singer later recalled, "was worth waiting for."

On the Road

While at the peak of her career, Marian Anderson traveled as many as six or seven months of the year—with short breaks of only a day or two in between performances. She was *not* a light packer, sometimes carrying more than twenty-five pieces of luggage at a time. From North to South, hot to cold, casual dress to concert gown, Marian made sure she had her wardrobe—and just about everything else—covered.

For her performances, Marian packed long evening gowns with accompanying shawls and shoes; outerwear might include coats, capes, gloves, hats, and boots or overshoes. There were day dresses and slacks, blouses and sweaters, shoes and slippers, handbags and scarves. Marian also carried a great deal of music with her. But besides these essentials, a set of Pyrex dishes, movie camera and film, electric hot plate, reel-to-reel tape recorder, radio, sleeping bag, towels, and an iron and small ironing board were just a few of the additional items this seasoned traveler's bags included at one time or another.

An accomplished seamstress, Marian occasionally even took her sewing machine with her, using it to make simple summer dresses and slacks. In between concert engagements on one tour, she even pinned, pleated, and stitched lined chintz curtains for her Connecticut home.

In her tours throughout Canada and the United States alone she sang on more than fifteen hundred stages in some six hundred cities to an estimated audience of more than six million.

The war's end also brought more opportunities for recordings, and Marian headed to the studio several times each year. "To tell the truth," she recalled, "I never liked the idea of singing into a microphone. I like to see faces before me."

In addition to her many appearances on the concert stage, Marian also sang on the radio and made numerous recordings throughout her career. This studio shot was taken in March 1951.

Nonetheless, Marian's recordings were tremendously popular, selling more than a million copies, with "Ave Maria" being one of the top favorites.

A Surprise Offer

While attending a social event in the fall of 1954, Marian was introduced to Rudolph Bing. It would prove to be a very important occasion for them both. Bing, then the general manager of New York's Metropolitan Opera, asked Marian if she would like to sing at the Met. Although the question was posed somewhat casually, Bing was *very* serious.

No African American singer had ever before appeared on the stage there, and it was well past time. However, Bing's request was not based on the color of Marian's skin but on her amazing abilities. As he had told a reporter several years before, "I am looking for the best, regardless of race or creed."

Marian was still surprised by the offer. Now in her late fifties and still incredibly talented, both she and her voice were somewhat past the age for an operatic debut. In addition, the role being considered was that of Ulrica, the sorceress in Verdi's opera *Un Ballo in Maschera* (*A Masked Ball*). While not a leading part, it was still extremely challenging.

Preparing to break through racial barriers once again, Marian stands on the Metropolitan Opera House stage with its general manager, Rudolph Bing, in 1954.

With Rudolph Bing (left) and Sol Hurok (right) at her side, Marian prepares to sign a contract with New York City's Metropolitan Opera Company in 1954, making her the first African American to appear on its stage.

After much thought, Marian agreed and signed a contract at the then-unheard-of figure of $1,000 per performance (about $7,500 by today's standards), which at that time was the highest ever paid by the Met. Within days after the announcement was made of Marian's impending debut, tickets for the first performance were sold out. Marian began serious rehearsals, not only of the music she would sing, but also the acting and movements for her role. Opening night was scheduled for January 7, 1955. From then on, the world of opera would never be the same.

CHAPTER 9

Applause and Acclaim

The chance to be a member of the Metropolitan has been a highlight of my life. It has meant much to me and to my people.

As the curtain rose on the second scene of Verdi's opera, Marian—in her role as the sorceress Ulrica—stood onstage mixing a brew in her cauldron. Marian was poised once again to make history and break barriers with the power of her voice. In addition to the singer's husband and family, the audience included distinguished guests such as Margaret Truman, Eleanor Roosevelt, and the Duchess of Windsor.

In costume for a dress rehearsal in 1955, Marian stirs her witches' brew as Ulrica, the sorceress in Giuseppe Verdi's opera *Un Ballo in Maschera* (*A Masked Ball*).

On January 7, 1955, Marian—with arms raised—makes her debut on the Metropolitan Opera stage. A standing ovation lasting nearly five minutes delayed the start of the scene.

At the sight of the famous contralto up onstage, the crowd went wild, erupting into a chorus of clapping and cheers lasting nearly five minutes. "I trembled," recalled Marian, "and when the audience applauded and applauded before I could sing a note I felt myself tightening into a knot. I had always assured people that I was not nervous about singing, but at that moment I was as nervous as a kitten."

It was a triumphant evening. Returning to her dressing room, Marian found numerous bouquets and more than two thousand congratulatory telegrams. Ever critical of her own abilities, she later wrote that she was not pleased with her first performance, feeling she "overdid" it. But not everyone agreed with her assessment. In the next day's *New York Times*, a prominent music critic wrote: "In Ulrica's one-half act, by her native sensibility, intelligence, and vocal art, Miss Anderson stamped herself in the memory and the lasting esteem of those who listened."

As before, Marian had opened a door, breaking down a barrier to her race, and she had done so with grace and dignity.

As before, Marian had opened a door, breaking down a barrier to her race, and she had done so with grace and dignity. Only three weeks after her debut performance, Robert McFerrin became the first African American baritone to sing at the Met. McFerrin had been a participant in the Met-sponsored "Auditions of the Air" program, where young singers could audition to become part of the opera company. The first prize was a contract with the Met, and McFerrin had won.

Biographers have debated whether his appearance may have been delayed in order that Marian—a much more famous and well-known African American figure—be the first to break the race barrier. Surely Marian's appearance onstage was guaranteed to generate less negative press and more positive support than an unknown performer. Regardless, there is no doubt that many factors were considered, in addition to Marian's musical talents, when the decision was made to invite her to perform the groundbreaking role.

Despite her busy concert schedule, Marian appeared as Ulrica in several more Met performances in New York, as well

The Metropolitan Opera

Founded in 1883 by a group of wealthy New York businessmen, the Metropolitan Opera has grown from a relatively small enterprise into one of the world's foremost companies. During its first few seasons, opera at the Met was performed strictly in Italian, then later in German, before settling on the current practice of performing most operatic works in their language of origin.

Some of the most famous musical artists of the time have graced the Met. In addition to Marian Anderson, they include the famed Italian conductor Arturo Toscanini; the internationally known tenor, Enrico Caruso, who appeared in a remarkable 863 performances; and stars like Roberta Peters, Luciano Pavarotti, Beverly Sills, and Placido Domingo.

Today, some 800,000 people attend more than two hundred performances of opera each year during the Met's regular season, and millions more experience the company on tour or via recordings and televised broadcasts. Originally located in a much smaller facility, the Met moved to its present home at New York City's Lincoln Center for the Performing Arts in 1966.

This is the original home of New York City's Metropolitan Opera House, c. 1912, at Broadway and 39th Street.

as in Cleveland, Boston, and her native Philadelphia. Not long after her final performance in the Verdi opera, Marian embarked on a tour of Israel, France, Spain, and North Africa. For Marian, her time spent in Israel was especially moving as she recalled childhood memories of her Jewish grandfather, Benjamin Anderson.

During several performances with the Israel Philharmonic, Marian sang Brahms's *Alto Rhapsody* in the Hebrew translation, thrilling audiences. In many of the African American spirituals she performed throughout her career, Marian sang of Jericho and its walls and of crossing the River Jordan. She visited both during her tour, and later recalled, "I could see in Israel the geographic places that represented the reality, and they stirred me deeply. I kept thinking that my people had captured the essence of that reality and had gone beyond it . . ."

Marian's Story

After this latest successful overseas tour, Marian—at Sol Hurok's urging—began to work with Harold Taubman on her autobiography. Despite revealing a few personal details—including the fact that she was a diehard Brooklyn Dodgers baseball fan—Marian was reluctant to open up to a stranger.

Taubman, a music writer for the *New York Times*, had difficulty getting Marian to express her feelings about prejudice and discrimination, and the experience was somewhat frustrating for them both. However, the end product, *My Lord, What a Morning*, was a critical success when it appeared in bookstores in 1956. Marian dedicated the volume to her mother, Anna.

Touring throughout the country and around the globe, Marian occasionally ended up in the same city as her good friend Eleanor Roosevelt. When that happened, the former first lady

Dressed somewhat elegantly for baking, Marian and her mother, Anna, pose for what was probably a publicity photo in the kitchen at Marianna Farm.

almost always rearranged her schedule so that she could attend at least one of the singer's performances. The two had enjoyed a steady correspondence since the late 1930s and continued their friendship until Eleanor Roosevelt's death in 1962. Once, when Marian finished performing in an auditorium where Mrs. Roosevelt was scheduled to give a lecture two days later, the singer left a message of welcome written in soap on the dressing room mirror.

Ambassador and Delegate

In 1957, Marian started out the year singing the national anthem at the second inauguration of President Dwight D. Eisenhower. Later that year, she was asked by the State Department to represent the United States on a nine-week goodwill tour throughout Southeast Asia. The tour would be the most extensive ever taken on by an American performer in that part of the world.

Guided by the U.S. Information Agency (a branch of the State Department), Marian's concert schedule was intertwined with numerous public appearances at schools, churches, and charity functions, as well as brief meetings with various government officials. As U.S. concern grew about the spread of Communism throughout Southeast Asia, it was hoped that Marian's appearances would generate positive interest in democracy.

Orpheus Fisher joined his wife on her nine-week goodwill tour of Southeast Asia in 1957. Here, a smiling Marian shakes hands in Hong Kong as a young bellhop looks on.

Accompanied by her husband, Franz Rupp, Isaac Jofe, and a team of documentary filmmakers, Marian logged some 35,000 miles, giving twenty-six performances in twelve countries. Now age sixty, the singer's voice did not have quite the strength and power that it once had. However, audiences were thrilled to hear Marian sing and recognized her natural warmth and generosity of spirit.

In 1958, Marian was appointed by President Eisenhower as an alternate U.S. delegate to the United Nations. Taking her responsibilities very seriously, she canceled all concert dates and other commitments while serving at the UN.

On one tour stop, to celebrate Malaysia's entry into the United Nations, Marian learned the Malaysian national anthem and sang it to a very appreciative audience. Her stop in New Delhi, like many others, was a huge success as enthusiastic fans quickly snapped up twelve hundred tickets for Marian's sell-out performance at that city's largest concert hall.

In December, after the singer's return to the United States, the one-hour documentary of the trip, entitled *The Lady from Philadelphia* was broadcast on CBS. Viewers loved it, and *Newsweek* magazine called the film "probably the most widely applauded show in TV history." Knowing of Marian's popularity with overseas fans, the State Department made arrangements for the film to be shown in nearly eighty countries around the globe.

Acknowledging her success as a goodwill ambassador for the United States, as well as her deep sense of patriotism, President Eisenhower asked Marian to serve as an alternate **delegate** to the United Nations in 1958. At first she was very hesitant to accept, feeling

After careful thought, Marian agreed to accept the position.

her background as a professional singer was poor preparation for so serious an assignment. Uncertain about what to do, Marian sought the advice of a close friend—Eleanor Roosevelt. After careful thought, Marian agreed to accept the position.

Postponing all concert appearances during her term, Marian took the assignment very seriously, serving on the Trusteeship Council, which oversaw eleven small trust territories hoping to achieve independence and self-governance. In many respects, Marian's role was primarily a symbolic and ceremonial one—she hosted receptions for various diplomats and read prepared statements regarding U.S. foreign policy. Although Marian was an

Marian (center) sings the national anthem on January 20, 1961, at John F. Kennedy's presidential inauguration. Four years earlier, she had also performed at President Eisenhower's inauguration.

alternate delegate, it was hoped that her very appearance at the UN would send a positive message to other countries regarding U.S. race-relations.

However, on one occasion she did speak out regarding a vote by the U.S. delegation on the future of what is now Cameroon. Criticized by some delegates for not taking a stand on African independence issues, Marian asked to speak. "There is no one in the room who is more interested in the people whose fate we are trying to determine than I," she passionately argued.

Approaching Retirement

By this time, Marian had been performing in public for more than half a century and had experienced a highly successful career. In 1961, she sang at the inauguration of President John F. Kennedy. Her voice—once strong and vibrant—now was less so. Music critics—some kindly, others not—began to mention the word "retirement" more and more. But Marian was not quite ready to give up the stage, instead traveling to New Zealand and Australia for a demanding two-month-long series of four separate concert programs in the spring of 1962.

The following year she performed in the South, where racial prejudice and personal humiliation had kept her from actively touring since the 1940s. In August of 1963, she returned to the Lincoln Memorial steps, the site of her historic 1939 performance. Joining Martin Luther King, Jr., and other participants, Marian sang "He's Got the Whole World in His Hands" for a crowd of more than 200,000 at the March on Washington.

> *Her voice—once strong and vibrant—now was less so. Music critics . . . began to mention the word "retirement" . . .*

Presidential Medal of Freedom

The nation's highest civilian honor, the Medal of Freedom was originated by President Harry S. Truman to recognize exceptional service to the country during wartime. Then, in 1963, President John F. Kennedy signed an executive order changing the award's name to the *Presidential* Medal of Freedom and broadening its scope to include "any person who has made an especially meritorious contribution to (1) the security or national interests of the United States, or (2) world peace, or (3) cultural or other significant public or private endeavors."

In addition to Marian Anderson, the first recipients Kennedy selected included the renowned cellist Pablo Casals, the writer and editor E. B. White (the author of *Charlotte's Web*), artist Andrew Wyeth, and Pulitzer Prize-winning author and playwright Thornton Wilder.

Sadly, President Kennedy was assassinated just weeks before the December ceremony. President Lyndon Johnson made the presentation of the awards in Kennedy's place.

On December 6, 1963, Marian Anderson was presented at the White House with the Presidential Medal of Freedom by Lyndon B. Johnson. The famed contralto was among the award's first recipients.

By now, Marian—and her voice—were ready to rest. She and Sol Hurok began to discuss announcing her retirement. Hurok, ever the showman, wanted to wait until just the right moment to notify the press. In the meantime, Marian was selected as a recipient of the Presidential Medal of Freedom, but the December 1963 awards ceremony was marred by deep sadness. President Kennedy had been assassinated just two weeks earlier. Days later, on December 12, Sol Hurok announced Marian's plans to retire. She would stop performing after a final tour, scheduled to begin in the fall of 1964. The farewell tour would conclude at New York's Carnegie Hall on Easter Sunday, 1965.

Marian's feelings about her final tour and upcoming retirement were put on hold as family concerns rose to the forefront. Anna Anderson, Marian's devoted mother and cherished companion, was ill. On January 10, 1964, she died of heart failure, at the age of eighty-nine. After the funeral, Marian coped

Prior to the start of her six-month farewell tour, she recorded several albums . . .

with her loss as best she could by devoting herself to her music. Prior to the start of her six-month farewell tour, she recorded several albums, including twenty-six emotionally charged African American spirituals, a number of which she had sung during her Philadelphia childhood more than a half-century earlier.

CHAPTER 10

Farewell

I have a great belief in the future of my people and my country.

Beginning with a sold-out concert appearance at Constitution Hall on October 24, 1964, Marian traveled to some fifty cities throughout North America on her farewell tour. On April 18, 1965, she gave her last performance; it, too, was a sell-out crowd. Standing on the stage of New York's Carnegie Hall—where she had performed more than fifty times in the past three decades—Marian gazed out at a star-studded audience that included some two hundred relatives and friends. At the conclusion of her program, when asked to do yet another encore, she told Sol Hurok, "No. It's finished."

On April 18, 1965, at the close of her farewell tour, Marian Anderson stands on the stage at Carnegie Hall once more. The six-month tour took Marian to some fifty cities on four continents.

Although the April Carnegie Hall appearance was billed as her "farewell performance," Marian had previously committed to a few more dates. The most important of these was an outdoor concert at the end of June with the Philadelphia Orchestra. Her twenty-eight-year-old nephew, James (Jimmy) DePreist, was conducting. Sadly, Marian's sister, Alyse Anderson, died just weeks before, but the singer refused to consider canceling her June performance, knowing how important it was for her nephew to have her there. In early July, Marian appeared again with Jimmy, when he conducted the Chicago Symphony Orchestra. It would be the last time she would ever sing in public.

A Voice Goes On

But Marian's mere presence was still compelling. Even if she no longer sang, she still drew large audiences, returning to the stage for more than a decade as the narrator of *A Lincoln Portrait*, American composer Aaron Copland's patriotic work that combined readings from Lincoln's famous speeches with traditional American folk tunes.

Traveling each season from Orlando to Buffalo, or St. Louis to Hollywood, she appeared with various conductors, among them her nephew, Jimmy, who was establishing a significant name for himself in the field of music. Marian also lectured at music schools and universities. In 1972, she spoke at the dedication of the Eleanor Roosevelt Wings of the Roosevelt Library in Hyde Park, New York.

The death of Sol Hurok in 1974 came as a huge shock to Marian and other members of the entertainment world. Despite the fact that he was in his eighties, Hurok had been such a presence in so many lives for so long that it was hard to imagine

James DePreist (born 1936)

As a young man, a career in music was never seriously considered for James DePreist. After all, the Anderson family already boasted a music star. "For a family that already had Marian Anderson," he once said, "it was like: 'We gave at the office.'"

However, "Aunt Marian" was always supportive of his music. In high school, he played in a band and formed a jazz quintet while at the University of Pennsylvania. In 1961, he traveled to Bangkok as an American specialist in music and played in a jazz band with Thailand's king. He also began conducting. While in Thailand, DePreist contracted polio.

Devoting himself to musical studies during his long—but successful—recovery, DePreist won the prestigious Dimitri Mitropoulous International Conducting Competition in 1964— the first American to do so. He then served as Leonard Bernstein's assistant conductor for the New York Philharmonic's 1965–1966 season.

In 1976, he became the Quebec Symphony's musical director. Four years later, he joined the Oregon Symphony. As its musical director for twenty-three seasons, DePreist is credited with that orchestra becoming one of the country's best. In 2005, he was awarded the National Medal of Arts by President Bush and accepted an appointment as conductor for the Tokyo Metropolitan Symphony Orchestra.

James DePreist with Marian Anderson in the 1960s. He followed his Aunt Marian with his own musical career.

Sol Hurok was the recipient of numerous honors and awards during his lifetime. His death in 1974 marked the end of a nearly forty-year partnership with Marian.

he was gone. At his memorial service, held at Carnegie Hall, a crowd of more than 2,600 people listened as Marian delivered the eulogy. "He was teacher, counsel, friend, and even more than that," she said. "He was the 'we' in all of us."

The following year, Orpheus Fisher suffered the first of a series of small strokes that would eventually leave him partially paralyzed. Expenses for her husband's care and the overall maintenance of Marianna Farm began to mount significantly. Marian made arrangements to sell their home and its acreage to a developer with the stipulation that she and her husband could remain there—as tenants—as long as they wished.

On February 27, 1977, Marian once again appeared at Carnegie Hall, this time for the star-studded celebration of her seventy-fifth birthday. Sensitive over her late graduation from high school, Marian had erased five years from her age during her professional career. What was billed as her seventy-fifth was, in actuality, her eightieth birthday.

Marian, appearing somewhat frail, graciously accepted the tributes paid to her that evening. These included the United Nations Peace Prize and the announcement by First Lady

After suffering from ill health for several years, Orpheus Fisher died in 1986. He and Marian (shown here in 1978) had shared more than forty years of marriage together.

Rosalynn Carter that a special gold medal had been authorized by Congress and was being struck in the singer's honor for her "untiring and unselfish devotion to the promotion of the arts in this country."

The awards continued to flow in. Despite her husband's failing health—and her own increasing frailty—Marian made a point of always trying to attend the various ceremonies. August 22, 1979, was proclaimed "Marian Anderson Day" by the city of Philadelphia, and the elderly singer was on hand for the festivities, which included the establishment of the Marian Anderson Library and Scholarship Fund at the University of Pennsylvania.

> . . . Marian made a point of always trying to attend the various ceremonies.

In 1984, she was named the first recipient of the Eleanor Roosevelt Human Rights Award. Attending the ceremony at New York's City Hall, Marian had to be helped from her wheelchair to the podium where she spoke briefly, thanking those attending. The invited guests' rendition of "He's Got the Whole World in His Hands" brought tears to Marian's eyes.

Final Years

After a decade of ill health, Orpheus "King" Fisher passed away on March 26, 1986. He and Marian had shared more than forty years of marriage. After the small memorial service, Marian toyed with the prospect of moving back to Philadelphia to live with her sister, Ethel, who still resided in the little house that Marian had helped to buy for her family many years before. But Marian, now used to the country life, opted to remain where she could see the trees and rolling hills on her farm.

Although she missed her husband's company, Marian was not lonely. Frequent visitors included her nephew, Jimmy, as well as a number of aspiring young African American performers like the famous Met sopranos Kathleen Battle and Jessye Norman. In many ways, Marian's life had made their own dreams possible.

In a photo taken shortly before her death at age 96, Marian poses with opera greats Jessye Norman (left) and Kathleen Battle (right). James Levine, the Metropolitan Opera's artistic director, stands in the center.

Saving Marian's Studio

Once a private retreat and rehearsal site for the famous contralto, Marian Anderson's Connecticut studio faced demolition in the 1990s after Marianna Farm was sold and subdivided. Only twenty-by-twenty-four feet in size, the cottage-like structure—with its distinctive "cove" ceiling—was designed by Orpheus Fisher, Marian's architect husband. In addition to the practice area, it also boasted a small kitchen, bathroom, and fireplace. Fisher's curved ceiling design produced an acoustically appealing space that mirrored the sound of a concert hall.

Spared the wrecking ball when preservationists came to the rescue, the compact building was relocated, fully restored, and opened to the public as a historic site in 2004. Exhibits and photographs highlight Marian's career and accomplishments, as well as her civic activities in the Danbury area.

Marian and Franz Rupp rehearse in the studio at Marianna Farm, 1951.

After the death of her sister Ethel in 1990, Marian realized it was time to think about leaving the isolation of her beloved Marianna Farm. With mixed emotions, Marian agreed in 1992 to move from Connecticut and live with Jimmy and his wife, Ginette, in Portland, Oregon. She seemed to adjust well to her new home, but after celebrating her ninety-sixth birthday on February 27, 1993, Marian's health began to seriously decline. On April 8, with her nephew at her side, Marian quietly slipped away.

Returning to her South Philadelphia roots, Marian Anderson was remembered at a memorial service held in June at Union Baptist Church. Speaking of "our Marian," the minister said, "We all have been blessed by her music of the soul, music that transcends time. The members of this church heard in that voice the grace and benediction that only God can give." Mindful of Marian's wish for "no fuss," Jimmy DePreist spoke simply, telling stories of the devotion his aunt had brought to his family and his life. At the conclusion of the service, a recording of Marian singing three of her favorite spirituals filled the church, leaving those attending the service inspired once more by the beauty of that glorious voice.

Marian's face adorns a postage stamp issued in her honor in 2005. First-day-of-issue ceremonies were held at Constitution Hall—the site from which she was once banned more than 60 years earlier.

Glossary

accompanist—someone who plays music along with a singer or singing group (usually on the piano).

Aryan—Nazi Party term used to describe white Western Europeans who have "pure" German blood.

auditions—trial performances used to determine an entertainer's skills.

chain gang—a group of prisoners chained together while working outdoors.

connotations—words or phrases that suggest an emotion or meaning.

credentials—documents or qualifications showing a person has certain skills or knowledge.

debut—a performer's first public appearance.

delegate—someone who is appointed or elected to represent others.

derogatory—indicating a low or negative opinion of something.

descendants—people who are relatives of a particular individual or group from the past.

encores—additional or repeated performances, usually requested by audiences.

exodus—journey made by a large group, usually to escape difficulty or danger.

Great Depression—period in U.S. history (1929 until about 1939) of serious economic failure and unemployment.

impresario—producer or manager of musicians or other entertainers.

"lost tribes" of Israel—ten tribes from ancient Israel who were captured by the Assyrians in 722 B.C. and mysteriously disappeared.

Nazism—political and economic system favoring superiority and loyalty to a strong leader; especially predominant in Germany from 1933–1945.

Passover—annual Jewish festival celebrating the Israelites' freedom from slavery in Egypt.

phonetically—representing sounds or relating to spoken language.

phonographic recording—sound waves copied onto a grooved plastic disc; sounds are replayed using a small needle (or stylus) that traces the grooves as the disc is rotated.

postlude—a closing piece of music that is played or sung.

prejudice—unfair or unkind attitude or "pre-judgment" about a person, group, or race.

racial discrimination—negative or abusive treatment based upon factors such as skin color, religion, or culture.

racism—the belief that one race is superior to another and that race determines character, abilities, or intelligence.

repertoire—for a musician, the songs or music that an artist is prepared to perform.

segregation—forced restriction or separation of a race or ethnic group from the rest of society.

Bibliography

Books

Anderson, Marian. *My Lord, What a Morning: An Autobiography*. Urbana and Chicago: University of Illinois Press, 2002.

Ferris, Jeri. *What I Had Was Singing: The Story of Marian Anderson*. Minneapolis: Carolrhoda Books, 1994.

Freedman, Russell. *The Voice That Challenged a Nation: Marian Anderson and the Struggle for Equal Rights*. New York: Clarion Books, 2004.

Keiler, Allan. *Marian Anderson: A Singer's Journey*. Urbana and Chicago: University of Illinois Press, 2002.

Meadows, James. *Marian Anderson: Journey to Freedom*. Chanhassen, MN: The Child's World, 2001.

Newman, Shirlee P. *Marian Anderson: Lady from Philadelphia*. Philadelphia: The Westminster Press, 1966.

Ryan, Pam Muñoz. *When Marian Sang: The True Recital of Marian Anderson*. New York: Scholastic Press, 2002.

Tedards, Anne. *Marian Anderson*. New York: Chelsea House Publishers, 1988.

Tobias, Tobi. *Marian Anderson*. New York: Thomas Y. Crowell Company, 1972.

Truman, Margaret. *Women of Courage*. New York: William Morrow and Company, Inc., 1976.

Vehanen, Kosti. *Marian Anderson: A Portrait*. Westport, CT: Greenwood Press, 1970.

Articles

Goodman, Walter. "Review/Television: Marian Anderson's Life of Unfailing Dignity." *The New York Times*, May 8, 1991.

Kozinn, Allan. "Marian Anderson Is Dead at 96." *The New York Times*, April 9, 1993.

Web Sites

Marian Anderson at the Met: The 50th Anniversary
http://www.metoperafamily.org/_post/education/marian-anderson/html/index.htm

Marian Anderson Historical Society http://www.mariananderson.org/

University of Pennsylvania Special Collections: Marian Anderson Papers
http://www.library.upenn.edu/collections/rbm/mss/anderson/anderson.html

Image Credits

About the Author

Victoria Garrett Jones is a freelance writer and former National Geographic Society researcher. The author of Sterling Biographies *Eleanor Roosevelt: A Courageous Spirit*, Jones lives with her husband and two children on Maryland's Eastern Shore. This is her sixth publication for Sterling Publishing.

Index

Accompanist, 29–30, 120. *See also* Boghetti, Giuseppe; King, Billy; Rupp, Franz; Vehanen, Kosti

Anderson, Anna Delilah Rucker
autobiography dedicated to, 103
death of, 111
Deep South trip, 25–26
in Europe, 56–58
family life, 5, 7
labor taking toll, 44–45
marriage to John, 3
photographs, 53, 104
relationship with, 17, 41
stressing education, 12, 17
traits of, in Marian, 22

Anderson, Benjamin, 2, 14–17, 104

Anderson, Isabella, 3, 10, 12

Anderson, John Berkley, 2, 3, 7, 10–12

Armstrong, Louis, 54

Aryan, 61, 120

Auditions, 30–32, 41–42, 101, 120

Autobiography, 103

Baby Contralto, 10–12

Bing, Rudolph, 97, 98

Birth, of Marian, 3

Black Jews, 16, 17

Boghetti, Giuseppe, 32–34, 36–37, 39, 41, 49

Carnegie Hall, 66, 91, 111, 112–113, 115

Chain gang, 11, 120

Choir, 7–9, 18–20

Connotations, 60, 120

Constitution Hall
ending segregation at, 93
performing at, 93, 112
turned away from, 71–76

Credentials, 7, 120

Daughters of the American Revolution (DAR), 71–76, 93

Death, of Marian, 119

Debut, 40, 120

Delegate, 107, 120

DePreist, Ethel and James, 53

DePreist, James (Jimmy), 68, 113, 114, 119

Derogatory, 27, 120

Descendents, 16, 120

Economic hardships, 49–52

Eleanor Roosevelt Human Rights Award, 116–117

Encores, 61, 80, 112, 120

Europe, 44–55
debut in, 48–49
financing concert in, 51–52
first studies in, 45–48
friends in, 46–48
further studies in, 50–51
meeting Toscanini, 61
performances in, 48–49, 51–52, 55, 56–58, 60–61, 103
Russian performance, 60–61
sailing to, 45, 50

Exodus, 6, 120

Family history, 2–12. *See also* Anderson, Anna Delilah Rucker
birth of Marian, 3
death of father, 13
growing up in Philadelphia, 4–7
home life, 5–7
Jewish influence, 15
love of music and, 7–10
making ends meet, 13–18
parents meeting/marrying, 3
relationship with grandfather, 14–17
sisters, 5, 9, 18, 43, 44, 53, 68, 78, 113, 119

Farewell tour, 112–113

Fisher, Orpheus "King," 105
courting Marian, 46, 52–53, 66, 86–87
ill health and death, 115, 116, 117
marriage to Marian, 94
marrying another woman, 39
meeting/attraction to, 29
studio designed by, 87, 118

Fisk Jubilee Singers, 11, 19

German lieders, 45, 47, 50, 51

Glossary, 120–121

Goodwill tour, 105–107

Great Depression, 49, 50, 52, 54, 120

Hayes, Roland, 18, 19, 33, 71

Howard University, 70–72, 76

Hurok, Sol
biographical sketch, 59
death of, 113–115
Lincoln Memorial performance and, 70, 71–72, 76–78, 80
managing career, 61, 62–63, 66–68, 91, 98
Marian hiring, 58–60
Marian marriage and, 94
Marian retirement and, 111

Impresario, 59, 120

Jews, 15, 16, 34, 59, 72, 77

Jim Crow laws, 24, 26, 27, 35, 49, 72

Judson, Arthur, 50, 52, 58

Kennedy, John F., 108, 109, 110

King, Billy, 29–30, 35, 40, 44, 50, 56, 58–60

King, Martin Luther, Jr., 109

Later years
final years, 117–119
losing family and friends, 111, 113–115, 117, 119
multiple awards, 115–117
speaking engagements, 113

Lincoln Memorial performances
day of, 78–80
dignitaries on platform, 78–79
events leading to, 76–78
impact of, 80–82
second, with Martin Luther King, Jr., 109

"Lost tribes" of Israel, 16, 120

Marian Anderson Scholarship Fund, 90

Marianna Farm, 87, 94, 104, 115, 118, 119

Marriage, to Orpheus Fisher, 94

Medal of Freedom, 110, 111

Migration, after Civil War, 6

Military performances, 88–89, 91

Mother. See Anderson, Anna Delilah Rucker

Mühlen, Raimund von Zur, 45, 46
Music studies
  with Agnes Reifsnyder, 24, 30
  in Europe, 45–48, 50–51
  experiencing prejudice and,
    20–22
  financial support for, 18–20,
    23–24, 33
  first voice lessons, 22–23
  German lieders and, 45, 47,
    50, 51
  with Giuseppe Boghetti,
    32–34, 36–37, 39, 41, 49
  with Mary Patterson, 22–23
  with Raimund von Zur
    Mühlen, 45, 46
My Lord, What a Morning, 103
NAACP (National Association for
  the Advancement of Colored
  People), 77, 83–84
National Association of Negro
  Musicians (NANM), 31
Nazism, 61, 120
New York Metropolitan Opera,
  97–98, 99–101, 102
Passover, 15, 16, 120
Pasternak, Joseph, 37–39
Patterson, Mary Saunders, 22–23
Payne, John, 45, 46
Performances. *See also* Lincoln
  Memorial performances
  Carnegie Hall, 66, 91, 111,
    112–113, 115
  church choir, 7–9, 18–20
  Constitution Hall, 93, 112
  in Deep South, 25–26
  economic hardships and,
    49–52
  in Europe, 48–49, 51–52, 55,
    56–58, 60–61, 103
  fame in Europe and America,
    56–58, 62–67
  goodwill tour and, 105–107
  honoring NANM, 31
  insults amidst, 91–92
  in Israel, 103
  for military personnel, 88–89,
    91
  New York Metropolitan
    Opera, 97–98, 99–101, 102
  New York Philharmonic

  competition and debut,
    41–43
  New York Town Hall, 39–41,
    63–65
  Philadelphia Academy of
    Music, 65
  as teen, 17–18, 24
  worldwide, 94–96, 103
Philadelphia, growing up in, 4–7
Philadelphia Medal, 88
Phonographic recording, 38, 120
Postage stamp, 119
Postlude, 56, 120
Prejudice, 20–22, 45, 91–93,
  103, 109, 120
Quilter, Roger, 46, 48
Racial discrimination, 21–22, 25,
  82, 91–92, 120
Racism, 76, 121
Raphael, Mark, 46, 48
Recordings, 37–39, 96–97
Reifsnyder, Agnes, 24, 30
Repertoire, 55, 121
Retirement. *See also* Later years
  farewell tour, 112–113
  preparing for, 111
  speaking engagements after,
    113
Robinson, Alexander, 7–8
Roosevelt, Eleanor
  award in honor of, 116–117
  biographical sketch, 75
  civil rights stand, 68–69, 75
  on first integrated seating at
    Constitution Hall, 93
  helping and befriending
    Marian, 72, 74–76, 99,
    103–105, 107
  inviting Marian to White
    House, 68–69
  presenting award to Marian,
    83–84
  resigning DAR membership,
    74–76
Rupp, Franz, 77–78, 84, 89,
  91, 92, 106, 118
Scholarship fund, 90
School. *See also* Music studies
  delayed, 17
  elementary, 9
  high school, 24, 26–29

  mother influence on, 12
Segregation, 25–26, 27, 72,
  93, 121
Sibelius, Jean, 56, 57, 65
Singing. *See also* Music studies;
  Performances
  evening gown for, 20
  love of music and, 7–10, 17
  for money, as teen, 17–18
  voice range, 7
  voice types and, 8
Sisters, 5, 9, 18, 43, 44, 53, 68,
  78, 113, 119
Southeast Asia goodwill tour,
  105–107
Spingarn Medal, 82–83
Spirituals
  family singing, 9
  Fisk Jubilee Singers and, 11,
    19
  at funeral, 119
  history of, 11
  performing, 43, 60–61, 65,
    80, 103
  recording, 37–38
Studio, of Marian, 87, 118
Timeline, iv
Toscanini, Arturo, 61, 62, 64, 79,
  102
Town Hall (New York), 39–41,
  63–65
Travel wardrobe and luggage, 95
Union Baptist Church, 7–8, 10,
  18–20, 33, 119
United Nations delegation,
  107–109
United Nations Peace Prize, 115
Vehanen, Kosti, 52, 56, 58–60,
  62, 63, 67, 69, 77–78, 80, 84,
  85
Voice. *See also* Performances;
  Singing
  range, in junior choir, 7
  training. See Music studies
  types, 8
White House performances/visits,
  68–69, 110
Wilson, Dr. Lucy Langdon,
  26–28, 30, 31–32